LifeAnswers

LIFEANSWERS
Making Sense of Your World

Ken Hemphill

*Personal Learning Activities
by Mike James*

LifeWay Press
Nashville, Tennessee

© Copyright 1993 • LifeWay Press
Reprinted 1995, 1997
All rights reserved

ISBN 0-8054-9964-4

Dewey Decimal Classification: 261
Subject Heading: CHRISTIANITY AND CURRENT ISSUES

This book is the text for course CG-0151
in the subject area Baptist Doctrine
in the Christian Growth Study Plan

Unless indicated otherwise, Scripture quotations
are from the Holy Bible,
New International Version, copyright 1973, 1978, 1984
by International Bible Society

Printed in the United States of America

LifeWay Press
127 Ninth Avenue, North
Nashville, Tennessee 37234

1: **Developing a Christian Worldview** 1

2: **Foundations for a Christian Worldview** 21

3: **What Is Our Origin?** 49

4: **What Am I Doing Here?** 75

5: **Why Does Evil Exist?** 99

6: **Where Am I Going?** 127

Bibliography 151

The Christian Growth Study Plan 152

Atheism: A negative worldview asserting that God does not exist.

Consistency: A belief system's ability to maintain its propositions without conflict among them.

Deism: A belief system that acknowledges God but denies His active involvement in the universe.

Enlightenment: A moment of significant insight in the process of personal or mystical self-discovery.

Existentialism: A belief system holding that a person is responsible for himself and to himself alone for what he becomes.

Integrity: A belief system's ability to deal truthfully and completely with all facts it encounters.

Monism: The belief that all is God and God is all.

New Age movement: A personal belief system combining elements of Eastern religions, mysticism, and modern psychology.

Nihilism: A belief system that rejects absolute grounds for objective reality or morality.

Panentheism: A belief system asserting that God is everything and everything is God but that God is more than the sum of all things.

Pantheism: A belief system asserting that God and the world are one.

Polytheism: A belief in many gods and a denial that one God deserves ultimate worship.

Practical relevance: A belief system's ability to meet real human needs and to solve real human problems.

Religious pluralism: The existence of many religions or belief systems in the same culture.

Secular humanism: An organized belief system asserting that humans are the center of the universe and denying God's existence.

Sufficiency: A belief system's ability to answer all of life's critical questions in a meaningful way.

Theism: A belief system grounded in the recognition of the one true God, the Creator and Sustainer of the universe.

Unity: A belief system's ability to unify all aspects of life and thought in a meaningful way.

Developing a Christian Worldview

It's a Mad, Mad, Mad, Mad World. Those classic words, the title of a once-popular movie, seem more appropriate today than at any other time. The newspaper and the television daily confirm our suspicion that the world has gone strangely out of orbit. Two teens murder their parents, who objected to their dating. A famous professional athlete dies of cancer, the direct result of steroid use. A decapitated body is found in a refuse dump. Rock musicians defy the law and all moral values, yet night after night they play to sold-out stadiums. Major religious denominations turn their backs on traditional biblical values. In a single week all of these stories appeared in the news.

How do we make sense of our world? Where do we find answers to the questions that really matter?

Life's Critical Questions
- ❏ What is life all about?
- ❏ Where did I come from?
- ❏ Why am I here?
- ❏ Where am I going?
- ❏ Does anybody care?
- ❏ Why does evil exist?
- ❏ Where can I find a source of strength?

▼THINK ABOUT IT

Check the critical questions above that trouble you the most. What other questions would you add to the list?

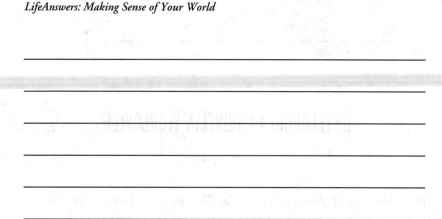

These questions relate to what is often called a worldview. If we listened to writers such as Jean-Paul Sartre, the French existentialist, we might conclude that the answers to these worldview questions do not exist. He "speaks of man as a bubble of consciousness in an ocean of nothingness, bobbing around until the bubble pops."[1] If that is an honest look at human life, we are nothing more than the punch line of a sick cosmic joke.

In this book we will take an honest look at life's ultimate questions and try to make sense of what appears to be a mad, mad, mad, mad world.

WHAT IS A WORLDVIEW?

Expressed simply, a worldview is the way we view the world and make our value judgments about life. How do we tie everything together as we think about life and death? How do we unify our vision of life? Our worldview is like colored glasses through which we look at the world about us. Those glasses affect our perception of everything we view. Thus, a worldview, whether Christian or secular, is the unifying perspective from which we organize our thinking about life, death, art, science, faith, learning, work, money, values, and morals. A worldview is our underlying philosophy of life. A worldview is where we go to look at the bottom line, to make sense of our world.

Many people do not think seriously about their worldview until a crisis causes them to question life. We hear cries like "If God is love, why did He let my little girl die?" Although we may think of that as a cry most often heard from a non-Christian, it is also asked by many Christians who do not have the spiritual resources to deal with tragedy.

Unfortunately, many Christians have never given their own worldviews serious consideration. For that reason, our understanding of life often is not consistent or unified. We allow the Bible to answer certain questions for us, but we often adopt the world's philosophy on other issues. Thus, we sometimes hear fellow church members ask the same questions the secular world asks— and with the same

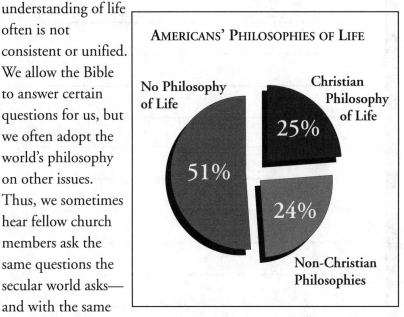

AMERICANS' PHILOSOPHIES OF LIFE

No Philosophy of Life

Christian Philosophy of Life

25%

51%

24%

Non-Christian Philosophies

degree of confusion. We have compartmentalized life, allowing our biblical faith to give us hope for eternal issues but ignoring it in practical matters such as finances, business relationships, moral values, and interpretations of world events. Many Christians do not even recognize a distinctively Christian view of such matters. In fact, Christians often adopt a totally secular worldview. Their way of looking at life is influenced more by movies, television shows, and popular songs than by the Bible. Thus, Christians too often find themselves unprepared to answer the critical questions of life.

▼HINK ABOUT IT

Do you have a worldview, a way of looking at life, or a philosophy of life? If so, write it here.

MY WORLDVIEW

_____

_____

_____

_____

_____

_____

_____

_____

_____

_____

_____

_____

_____

_____

_____

WHY DO WE NEED A WORLDVIEW?

Every believer needs to develop a worldview based on God's Word. Let me suggest six practical reasons why.

A worldview helps us integrate biblical principles with daily life. It gives substance to our values and gives unity and integrity to our thinking. It provides guidance for making clear choices when confronted with new and unfamiliar situations. A worldview enables us to apply our beliefs and confessions to our behavior.

A clear understanding of the biblical worldview provides a foundation for and gives substance to our faith. We need to know not only what we believe but also why we believe it. For example, what is the basis for our conviction about family values? Can we defend the Christian life-style? Do we have a right to suggest that our values are better than or more correct than another person's values? Our worldview should have a profound effect on our thinking about issues such as sexual practices, abortion, euthanasia, the homeless, and the environment.

A clear understanding of our worldview is essential because of an overt challenge from the secular world. One does not have to look far to find challenges to the Christian worldview. "No generation in the history of human thought has seen such swift and radical inversion of ideas and ideals."[2] For example, universities that were founded to teach values grounded in divinely related commandments have not only banned those values from the classroom but also, in some cases, have embraced values that directly oppose biblical revelation. Some courses in science, history, and psychology dismiss the idea of God, regarding it as irrelevant.

A coherent worldview gives us a more effective witness in the marketplace. Many Christians do not witness because they are afraid they will be asked questions they cannot answer and will be embarrassed. In turn, many thinking non-Christians have refused to take the gospel seriously because no one has presented the facts clearly and cogently. They associate faith with believing in spite of the facts or even with believing what cannot be true. If we understand the basis of our own faith, we can view the questions and objections of our secular friends as opportunities for witnessing rather than as stumbling blocks.

A clear understanding of the Christian worldview is essential because the world has become our neighborhood. When I was a child, all the people who followed non-Christian religions lived in faraway countries. Today nearly everyone has a neighbor who is from another country or religious background. We now know and do business with Buddhists, Hindus, Muslims, and others. Recently, this fact was brought home to me graphically. I was walking between my house and the one next door when the smell of incense wafted from the window, accompanied by a lilting chant. I knew that my new neighbors were Indian, but I was nonetheless surprised to learn that they have a household shrine, complete with a stone god. Imagine—idolatry next door to a Baptist preacher! A few years ago we would not have thought it possible. Not only has cultural migration created a new religious pluralism, but today's New Age emphasis has also introduced many Eastern mystical thoughts into America's marketplace. The Friday, July 12, 1991, edition of *USA TODAY* featured an article titled "Spiritual Life-styles of the Rich and Famous." The article featured the many Hollywood personalities who are committed to New Age thinking, following the many paths to enlightenment. Television has brought pagan religious ideas into our living rooms, so that whether we live in a metropolitan area or in rural America, we live in a world neighborhood.

We must clearly understand the Christian worldview because it is commanded in Scripture. It is not only a good idea for believers to be able to give a reasonable account of their convictions but also a direct command in Scripture. First Peter 3:15 states, "Always be prepared to give an answer to everyone who asks you to give the reason for the hope that you have."

THINK ABOUT IT

Read again each reason for developing a worldview. Then number the reasons in order of importance for your life now.

___ A worldview helps us integrate biblical principles with daily life.

___ A clear understanding of the biblical worldview provides a foundation for and gives substance to our faith.

___ A clear understanding of our worldview is essential because of an overt challenge from the secular world.

___ A coherent worldview gives us a more effective witness in the marketplace.

___ A clear understanding of the Christian worldview is essential because the world has become our neighborhood.

___ We must clearly understand the Christian worldview because it is commanded in Scripture.

Mark your response on each continuum.

1. How mature is your faith?

   Immature   *Mature*

   1   2   3   4   5   6   7   8   9   10

2. How confident are you about explaining your faith to an unbeliever?

   Unconfident   *Confident*

   1   2   3   4   5   6   7   8   9   10

3. How willing are you to share your faith with an unbeliever?

   Unwilling   *Willing*

   1   2   3   4   5   6   7   8   9   10

WHAT DO COMPETING WORLDVIEWS CLAIM?

We are being literally bombarded by the claims of competing worldviews. Movies, television, and print media highly publicize non-Christian worldviews. Shirley MacLaine's revelation of her involvement with the occult was greeted at first by a smirk that suggested, "Well, that's Hollywood." But her books and her extensive public-speaking itinerary have caused many to view her with alarm, while others see her as a spiritual leader. But it is not just the Shirley MacLaines of Hollywood fame who promote competing worldviews.

Our nine-year-old daughter, Katie, was recently given an assignment by her teacher at her Christian school to collect overt references to other worldviews, particularly the occult. Katie—not to mention her parents—was amazed to discover the widespread references to a mystical worldview in our culture. They are found frequently on popular sitcoms and in newspaper advertisements, even for businesses like banks and car dealerships. A local radio station reports on traffic as if viewing the scene through a crystal ball. Although done in jest, it is a not-too-subtle reminder that we confront competing worldviews daily.

Because this book is primarily concerned with developing a Christian worldview, we will not give much attention to other worldviews. Other books on this subject, such as the ones listed in the bibliography, address such matters in greater detail. If you look at those books, you will discover that some authors list three competing philosophical systems, while others list five or six. Often, the actual number of world systems listed depends on whether the author considers a particular thought system to be encompassed by a larger system. Do not be overly concerned if you find this a bit confusing. Because of such overlaps we will not attempt to give an extensive or exhaustive list, but the following chart lists some of the more prominent worldviews, some of which are then overviewed in the material that follows the chart. This book also provides enough information for you to understand the potential impact of different worldviews. Its goal is not to refute the alternative views but to build the case for the Christian worldview.

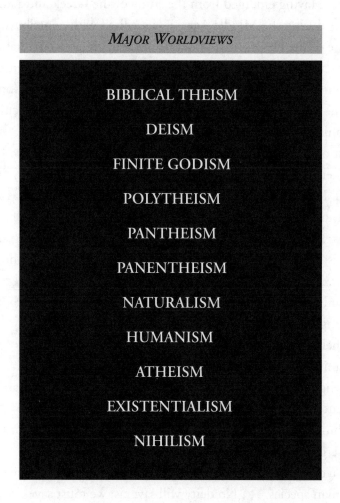

MAJOR WORLDVIEWS

BIBLICAL THEISM

DEISM

FINITE GODISM

POLYTHEISM

PANTHEISM

PANENTHEISM

NATURALISM

HUMANISM

ATHEISM

EXISTENTIALISM

NIHILISM

Atheism

This view is a negative worldview, asserting that God does not exist. It is the negation of theism, or the biblical worldview. In 1963 the Supreme Court ruled that some atheistic religions exist, listing secular humanism among them. *Humanism* is somewhat difficult to define because it is used in many different ways in various contexts. *Humanism,* purely defined, refers to a system of thought or action concerned only with the interests and ideals of people. Having emerged from the study of the Greek and Latin classics during the Middle Ages, it is credited with contributing to the rise of the Renaissance. Because all of us are concerned about the interests and ideals of people, we are, in the broadest sense, humanists. But in our day humanism, devoid of belief in God, has become a belief system. As such, it is often referred to as secular humanism or scientific humanism. Holding to a purely evolutionary view of life, it rejects a supernatural worldview. Its basic tenets are that persons are part and product of the physical world. Individuals determine their values, based on what has value or meaning for humankind. Persons become the measure of all things. It is a person-centered religion. All sense of meaning and hope is invested in nature and humanity and is limited to those realms. Because leading educators such as John Dewey held to a humanistic worldview, students are often influenced by the teaching of humanism in our public schools and colleges.[3]

Atheism as a religious worldview is best seen in secular humanism, which lists the following among its beliefs.

- "Religious humanists regard the universe as self-existing and not created."
- "Humanism believes that man is a part of nature and that he has emerged as the result of a continuous process."
- "We can discover no divine purpose or providence for the human species. . . . No deity will save us; we must save ourselves."[4]

Pantheism

Pantheism is a worldview based on the concept that God and the world are one. The universe, conceived of as a whole, is God. This worldview, which underlies many Eastern religions, has made its way into Western society through Christian Science and the New Age movement, emphasizing channeling, meditation, yoga, and other Eastern religious practices. Its central focus is monism, which asserts that all is God and God is all. Many secular ecology movements lean toward a form of pantheism, especially when they personalize the universe and place natural or animal needs equal to or above human needs.

Panentheism

This view claims that God is in everything and that everything is in God; but unlike pantheism, it holds that God is more than the universe. This view attempts to offer a compromise between pantheism and theism. God is thought of as developing and changing along with the world. Panentheism is encountered in modern process theology, which suggests that the world and God are both in process, or flux. God is seen not as perfect but as being in the process of perfection.

Deism

This word comes from the Latin word for God, *deus*. This view, while acknowledging the existence of God, sees Him as an absentee landlord. He is not actively involved in the affairs of humanity. God started everything in creation, setting natural laws in place, but refuses to interfere. Thus, a deist denies the miraculous and looks to the sufficiency of human reason. Deism, as a worldview, is no longer a major factor; but its influence is still felt, particularly in some departments of religion in educational institutions.

Polytheism

Polytheism is the belief that many gods exist and that no one God deserves ultimate worship. You may be familiar with the gods of ancient Greece and Rome but may be surprised to find that polytheism still survives. In fact, interest in polytheistic religion, sometimes called new paganism, is growing. Geisler and Brooks state that the largest and fastest-growing polytheistic religion in America today is Mormonism. They quote from the Mormon *Book of Abraham*: "The Lord said: Let us go down. And they went down at the beginning, and they, that is the gods, organized and formed the heavens and the earth."[5]

Theism

Theism, from the Greek word for God, *theos*, is grounded in a belief in the existence of one God, who is the Creator of the universe. The world depends on God for its existence, but the universe is not divine. God operates the world through natural laws but can intervene at any time in the affairs of humankind. Christianity, Judaism, and Islam are theistic religions.

▼HINK ABOUT IT
Match each worldview with its belief about God.

___ 1. Atheism   a. God is developing or in process.

___ 2. Pantheism   b. God does not exist.

___ 3. Panentheism   c. Many gods exist.

___ 4. Deism   d. God exists but is not involved in

___ 5. Polytheism   the world.

___ 6. Theism   e. There is one God, the Creator and

                         Sustainer of all.

                  f. The universe is God.

Answers: 1. b, 2. f, 3. a, 4. d, 5. c, 6. e.

WHERE DO WE BEGIN?
The questions of where to begin and what evidence to examine are good ones to begin with. Christians are often intimidated by the

suggestion in the marketplace that the Christian worldview is not intellectually viable because it is based on certain presuppositions, such as the existence of God and the reliability of the Bible as the Word of God. Does our acceptance of these beliefs constitute a weakness in our system?

No, it does not! The truth is that every worldview is based on a set of presuppositions. Anyone who thinks about life does so with certain presuppositions. No scientist can prove a clear link between his theories of life's origin and nature's actual condition in the beginning. Because the scientist was not present at the beginning of time, he must base his theories on certain faith presuppositions about the beginning of life and about the existence of matter. These faith presuppositions, or axioms, will affect the way he interprets other information that is gathered. For example, the conclusion one derives from carbon-dating techniques, which are used to determine the age of a bone or a plant fossil, will be affected by one's assumption about the age of the earth. If one begins with the belief that the earth is billions, rather than thousands, of years old, then one may reach a different conclusion than his colleague, even though the data are the same for both researchers.

"Euclid's classic work on *The Elements*, written about 300 B.C., stated the five postulates or unproved principles concerning lines, angles, and figures from which he deduced geometry." From the five postulates "he adduced five other unproved principles, called axioms." From his postulates, axioms, and definitions he formulated the theorems used in mathematics today. Thus, math has certain axioms that must be accepted and learned before one can proceed with its study.[6]

We should not apologize for having certain axioms or presuppositions on which we base the reasoning for our understanding of the world. Carl F. H. Henry, the longtime editor of *Christianity Today* and one of the foremost thinkers of our time, has stated: "The fact is, nothing will set the mind adrift more fruitlessly than the absence of all postulates; indeed, such absence leads to mindlessness in less time than it takes to think. In short, without faith neither science nor philosophy nor theology can make progress."[7]

▼THINK ABOUT IT

Define the term *axiom* in your own words.

_____

_____

Explain the relationship between our faith presuppositions and our worldview.

_____

_____

_____

_____

Do you think that the presence of certain presuppositions weakens a worldview? Why or why not?

_____

_____

_____

_____

Some critics argue that the Christian worldview is circular because it begins with what first needs to be proved. But this same objection would apply equally to all systems, "since no system exists without basic axioms."[8] Thus, we can agree that all worldviews are based on basic faith presuppositions. This is neither a liability nor an asset, simply a statement of fact. How, then, are we to make any judgment about the "right" or "accurate" worldview?

How Do We Test Worldviews?

Do we have a basis for testing our worldview or that of another person? Must we simply accept the popular notion that one worldview is as good as the next? If so, then our efforts to teach our worldview to our children might be inappropriate, and our efforts to spread the Christian worldview through evangelism expend misplaced energy. We are left with little more than an anemic revelation: the suggestion that all knowledge is in flux and that we must accept the truth in all worldviews. Such an idea is often promoted under the guise of tolerance. However, we must recognize that Jesus and the authors of Scripture claimed exclusivity:

- " 'I am the gate; whoever enters through me will be saved' " (John 10:9).
- " 'I am the way and the truth and the life. No one comes to the Father except through me' " (John 14:6).
- " 'Salvation is found in no one else, for there is no other name under heaven given to men by which we must be saved' " (Acts 4:12).

If every worldview must be evaluated, how do we go about that task? A worldview must pass five tests: sufficiency, unity, consistency, integrity, and practical relevance. If a particular worldview passes these tests, proving to be a comprehensive system of truth, then it *alone* must be correct. For if it truly is comprehensive, then every other system must contain contradictions and must therefore be false. The bottom line is that only one system can be correct. If 2 plus 2 equals 4, then any other answer must be false.

TESTING WORLDVIEWS

- ❑ Sufficiency
- ❑ Unity
- ❑ Consistency
- ❑ Integrity
- ❑ Practical Relevance

Sufficiency

The first and most obvious test is a system's ability to answer all of the critical questions of life in a meaningful way. Does it explain all of life, and does it answer questions arising from life's experiences?

Many views are invalidated by their inability to explain the issues of life fully. Some may give solutions for one or two questions but fail to account for the remaining critical questions. I contend that only Christianity integrates beliefs with life, providing valid answers to all of life's critical questions.

Unity

The credibility of a worldview depends on its capacity to unify all aspects of life and thought in a meaningful way. Does it cohere, or must we look to other systems for partial answers? Can our worldview enable us to integrate all of our thinking about life?

Consistency

Truth, by definition, should be consistent with itself. Any viewpoint that has inconsistent propositions destroys its own credibility. Carl F. H. Henry has illustrated inconsistency in the humanist agenda of social ethics. The attempt to layer ethics onto a naturalistic worldview has created "a philosophical monstrosity that defies logical consistency."[9] A system that argues that personality is just an accident of unthinking, impersonal forces cannot consistently argue that persons are bound by enduring duties. "The inconsistency of the humanist is perhaps most apparent in his response when he is wronged by a fellow human being." He must assume that another's action is wrong and that his response is correct; yet that is inconsistent with his own worldview.[10]

Integrity

Does a particular worldview deal with facts truthfully and completely? If we have to deny known facts or create nonfacts to defend our worldview, then it fails the test of integrity. We must distinguish here between fact and theory. Evolution is a theory, not a fact. The Christian worldview may not accept the theory of evolution but still has integrity because it can adequately deal with the scientific facts.

Practical Relevance

Is the worldview relevant? Does it actually meet deepest human needs and solve human problems? Does it provide purpose and direction for human life? Can it help us deal with our guilt, establish meaningful relationships, and relate rightly to the world? If I live by this worldview, will it produce ethical fruitfulness?[11]

Christianity alone can satisfy these criteria, and in this book we will look at the real issues of life. We will ask how other worldviews answer questions such as, Why am I here? and, Why does evil exist? Can the Christian worldview provide sufficient, unified, consistent, and practical answers without ignoring or creating facts?

▼HINK ABOUT IT

Complete each sentence by using one of the five terms that test a worldview: *sufficiency, unity, consistency, integrity,* or *practical relevance.*

1. When a worldview deals with all facts truthfully and completely, it has _____.
2. When a worldview answers the questions of life in a meaningful way, it has _____.
3. When a worldview does not contradict itself, it has _____.
4. When a worldview addresses the deepest human problems, it has _____ _____.
5. When a worldview is coherent, it has _____.

Answers: 1. integrity, 2. sufficiency, 3. consistency, 4. practical relevance, 5. unity.

---

[1]Arthur F. Holmes, *Contours of a World View* (Grand Rapids: Eerdmans, 1983), 12.

[2]Carl F. H. Henry, *The Christian Mindset in a Secular Society* (Portland: Multnomah, 1984), 81.

[3]For an excellent discussion of humanism see Arthur F. Holmes, *Contours of a World View*, 15-30.

[4]Paul Kurtz, ed., *Humanist Manifestos I and II* (Buffalo: Prometheus Books, 1973), 8, 16.

[5]Norman L. Geisler and Ronald M. Brooks, *When Skeptics Ask* (Wheaton: Victor Books, 1990), 54.

[6]Carl F. H. Henry, *Toward a Recovery of Christian Belief* (Wheaton: Crossway Books, 1990), 63. Read Henry's book for a clear understanding of basic axioms in formulating thought.

[7]Ibid., 44.

[8]Ibid., 90.

[9]Henry, *Christian Mindset*, 87.

---

¹⁰Ibid.

¹¹For a more complete discussion of tests for a worldview, see Jerry H. Gill, *On Knowing God: Directions for the Future of Theology* (Philadelphia: Westminster, 1981), 144, and L. Russ Bush, *A Handbook for Christian Philosophy* (Grand Rapids: Zondervan, 1991), 81-91. Gill gives three guidelines: comprehensive coherence, internal consistency, and ethical fruitfulness. Bush suggests logical or rational consistency, empirical adequacy, and explanatory.

Agnosticism: The belief that God may or may not exist.

Axiological argument: The argument for God's existence based on the moral order present throughout the human experience.

Axioms: Foundational, propositional, self-evident truths.

Cosmological argument: The argument for God's existence based on the existence of the universe.

General revelation: The theological affirmation that creation and moral "oughtness" point to God's existence.

Inerrancy: The absolute truthfulness of the Bible as Scripture.

Infallibility: The full trustworthiness of the Bible as Scripture.

Inspiration: The transmission of the content of the Bible as Scripture from God to humanity through persons.

Ontological argument: The argument for God's existence based on reason or the universality of the idea of God.

Resurrection: Jesus Christ's act of returning to life after His death, never to die again.

Special revelation: The theological affirmation that Jesus Christ and the Bible point directly to God's existence and nature.

Teleological argument: The argument for God's existence based on the design and order of the universe.

Foundations for a Christian Worldview

Whether or not we know it, we all think with basic presuppositions. When we got out of bed this morning, we did certain things that were based on presuppositions we believe to be absolute. We got dressed and combed our hair because we believe that we actually exist. If we are nothing more than a figment of our imagination, why bother to dress? We hold certain universal and basic beliefs in common with virtually anyone:

Belief in our own existence. It would be futile to defend the idea that nothing exists, including ourselves, since there would be no one to hear or make the defense. To suggest that nothing exists is absurd.

Belief in a real, external world that is orderly and noncontradictory. If we argue that the real world exists but is contradictory, then any attempt to make sense of it is futile from the outset, since it is contradictory by definition.

Belief in the existence of an ultimate reality. If no ultimate reality exists, then life has no meaning or purpose. We are really a cosmic joke, and worse, there was no one who uttered the joke.[1]

Every worldview adds to these fundamental beliefs other truths that are specific to the particular thought system. The foundational truths on which we build our worldview are sometimes referred to as axioms.

What, then, are the axioms—foundational, self-evident truths—that form the basis for the Christian worldview? They are listed in the following illustration.

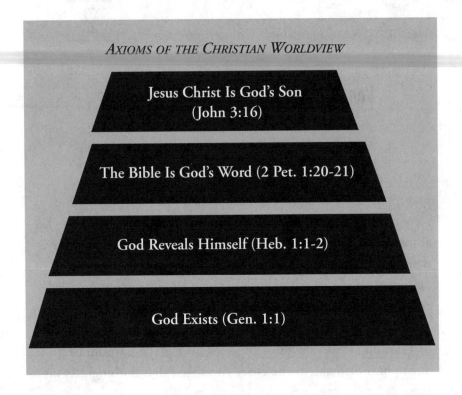

AXIOMS OF THE CHRISTIAN WORLDVIEW

Jesus Christ Is God's Son
(John 3:16)

The Bible Is God's Word (2 Pet. 1:20-21)

God Reveals Himself (Heb. 1:1-2)

God Exists (Gen. 1:1)

AXIOM 1: GOD EXISTS

When we consider God's existence, we have only three possible options.

1. God does not exist (atheism).
2. God may or may not exist (agnosticism).
3. God exists (theism).

The Bible begins with the words "In the beginning God" (Gen. 1:1). God's existence is a fundamental axiom of the Christian worldview. The implications of a belief in God are far-reaching, affecting our thinking and our values. We become accountable to God for our life and thus for our conduct.

Can we prove that God exists? We certainly cannot put God in a test tube and prove that He exists. But neither can we put George Washington, Abraham Lincoln, or any historical character under a microscope and prove that he existed. History cannot be repeated and therefore cannot be proved through the scientific method. Some realities, such as historical events and feelings like love and joy, cannot be proved by the scientific method, but this does not disprove their reality. But while acknowledging that God's existence cannot be proved by the scientific method, it is equally important to note that God cannot be disproved by the scientific method. To disprove God's existence, one would have to be in all places at all times in history. If we could accomplish that task, we would qualify for divinity.

▼THINK ABOUT IT

Mark the following statements *T* for true or *F* for false.

___ 1. God's existence can be proved by the scientific method.
___ 2. A belief in God's existence has profound implications for a person's values.
___ 3. To disprove God's existence would require that a person be divine.

Answers: 1. F, 2. T, 3. T.

Although we cannot prove historical events, we can find evidence of them, which is a key aspect of the scientific method. Thus, we can examine the evidence of God's existence. Four basic arguments for God's existence have been presented.[2]

The Argument from Creation

Since the universe now exists, it must have come from something. Atheistic evolutionists argue that the universe is eternal, but scientific evidence itself refutes that claim. The law of biogenesis states that life begets life. The second law of thermodynamics observes that things left to themselves move from order to disorder. Thus, the existence of matter and of the world itself points to the existence of a higher power or Creator. This argument from creation is called the cosmological argument, from the Greek word *cosmos,* meaning *orderly world.*

The Argument from Design

Since the universe demonstrates design and order, it is reasonable to conclude that behind it stands a great Designer. It is unthinkable to us that a beautiful, complex building can exist without an architect and a builder. Yet some scientists argue that chance and adequate time are sufficient to account for the obvious order of the universe. However, many see the absurdity of such a suggestion. "One scientist figured the odds for a one-cell animal to emerge by pure chance at 1 in $10^{40,000}$."[3] Obviously, the odds for the chance occurrence of a creature with the complexity of a human being are infinitely higher. The probability that our universe happened by chance has been compared to the possibility that a tornado could sweep through a junkyard and create a functional 747 jet.[4] Even Charles Darwin stated in *The Origin of Species,* "To suppose that the eye [with so many parts working together] could have been formed by natural selection, seems, I freely confess, absurd in the highest degree."[5] Carl Sagan, discussing the human brain, admitted that it has "the circuitry of a machine more wonderful than any devised by humans."[6] The argument from design is called the teleological argument, from the Greek word *telos,* meaning *purpose.*

The Argument from Moral Law

This argument is based on the moral order of the universe. It begins with the observation that in all cultures and in all periods of history, people have been conscious of an objective moral order. This law deals with what ought to take place in society. Various cultures, for example, may differ on the number of wives a man should marry; but we agree that no man can marry any woman he chooses, particularly if he chooses someone else's wife. Universally, we find that people appeal to some pattern of accepted behavior. We hear it in phrases such as "That's my seat," "Come on, you promised," or "What if someone did that to you?" C. S. Lewis's classic defense of Christianity, *Mere Christianity,* clearly presents this view. It is also called the axiological view, from the Greek word *axios,* meaning *value* and *judgment.*

The Argument from Being

This view states that God must exist by definition. Thus, it is an argument from reason. Since universally we have the idea of God in our minds, God must exist not only subjectively in the mind but also objectively outside the mind. The God who exists objectively behind the idea is the most perfect Being conceivable. Perhaps you have heard the famous reference to the "God-shaped vacuum" in everyone's heart. This ontological argument is so called because it comes from the Greek word *ontos,* which means *being.*

To these classical arguments we could add the argument of cause and effect. We know that every effect has a prior cause. Humans and the material universe are effects that had a cause. If we go back far enough, we must of necessity come to the uncaused cause. The question "Who caused or created God?" is illogical because God is the truly original cause. God needs no cause because only finite, contingent beings need a cause and creator. Christians believe that the uncaused Cause is the God of Scripture, who reveals Himself as YHWH (Jehovah): " 'I AM WHO I AM' " (Ex. 3:14). Some translators prefer "I CAUSE TO BE THAT WHICH I CAUSE TO BE." Further, we can point to persons over the centuries whose lives have been changed by their personal experiences with God.

Although these arguments do not actually prove God, they provide strong evidence for God's existence and activity. The skeptic must honestly confront this cumulative evidence.

▼THINK ABOUT IT

The writer has presented four arguments for God's existence.
Match them with their definitions.

___ 1. The argument from creation (cosmological)

___ 2. The argument from design (teleological)

___ 3. The argument from moral law (axiological)

___ 4. The argument from being (ontological)

a. The idea of God exists universally in every culture; therefore, God exists.

b. The material existence of a created universe demands that God exists.

c. The universe demonstrates design and order; therefore, God exists.

d. The commonality of some form of moral values and judgments points to God's existence.

Answers: 1. b, 2. c, 3. d, 4. a.

Certain implications are obvious from the conclusion that a sovereign Creator God exists:

- As creatures, we are subject to God.
- God has the answers to questions that are beyond our knowledge because He alone was there from the beginning.
- God has the authority to set the parameters for living our lives.

AXIOM 2: GOD REVEALS HIMSELF

It is not enough to say that God exists. We must then ask if He can be known and how. A central axiom of the Christian worldview is that God has chosen to reveal Himself to humanity. This belief sets Christianity apart from most other worldviews and world religions that chronicle humanity's attempt to find God. The Bible is a Book not about humankind's quest for God but about God's passion to save humans. When Adam sinned in the garden, he did not look for God. God sought Adam.

The stirring affirmation of Scripture is "Thus says the Lord." If we assert that God is active in creating us, we further affirm that He is active in our knowing, especially in our knowing Him. The Bible teaches that the creation itself and the human sense of moral "oughtness" bear witness to God. We refer to these evidences as *general revelation.* Paul began the Book of Romans by referring to God's revelation of Himself through creation (see 1:20) and through the human conscience (see 1:19; 2:14-15).

Yet God did not leave people to discover Him only through general revelation. He revealed Himself far more explicitly through His redemptive work, made fully known in Jesus Christ: "In the past God spoke to our forefathers through the prophets at many times and in various ways, but in these last days he has spoken to us by his Son, whom he appointed heir of all things, and through whom he made the universe" (Heb. 1:1-2). God has also revealed Himself more fully through the Bible. Jesus and the Bible are expressions of God's *special revelation.* Notice that the initiator and actor in revelation is God.

THINK ABOUT IT
Mark two kinds of general revelation with a *G* and two kinds of special revelation with an *S.*

__ Inspiration   __ The Bible

27

___ Jesus   ___ Archaeology
___ Moral oughtness   ___ Creation

Moral oughtness and creation are examples of general revelation. *Special revelation* refers to Jesus and the Bible.

Axiom 3: The Bible Is God's Word

The Bible, the written record of God's revelation of Himself to persons, is crucial to our understanding of God and the world He created. Not only is the Bible important for adding theology to our general knowledge, but it is also central to all knowledge, for in it we encounter the God who acts. The Bible is the most complete source of our knowledge about God. It is consistent to speak of Christ as the living Word of God and the Bible as the written Word of God.

Throughout the history of the church, leaders have spoken of Scripture as the only final and sufficient rule of faith. For this reason Scripture becomes the final authority, the point of reference by which all beliefs and behavior must be evaluated. This authority extends to every area of life,[7] becoming the basis for all else we will discuss about life and relationships. On the centrality of Scripture to the worldview process Carl F. H. Henry wrote, "Apart from the Bible no firm reply exists against the rampant unbelief and strident skepticism of our age, no sure way around the contorted detours of modern culture, no lasting alternative to the extraordinary evils that plague our generation."[8]

How Does God Speak?

How would infinite God speak to finite humans? We have already noted that in Romans 1 Paul stated that God reveals Himself in nature and through the human conscience. Both the Old and New Testaments tell the story of God's redemptive activity in history. This is another way God revealed Himself.

Further, the writer of Hebrews indicated that God spoke through the prophets and through His Son. And in 2 Peter 1:20-21 we read: "Above all, you must understand that no prophecy of Scripture came about by the prophet's own interpretation. For prophecy never had its origin in the will of man, but men spoke from God as they were carried along by the Holy Spirit." The Bible, the written Word of God, is God's revelation of Himself, given to us to enable us to know God and live by His standards. This is precisely the point Paul made in 2 Timothy 3:16-17: "All Scripture is God-breathed and is useful for teaching, rebuking, correcting and training in righteousness, so that the man of God may be thoroughly equipped for every good work."

What Does the Bible Say About Itself?
Although the Bible's claims about itself as God's Word cannot be said to constitute proof, they are relevant and significant claims that are supported by substantial evidence. Therefore, they must not be ignored.

> The Bible . . .
> - is God's revelation
> - is inspired
> - is trustworthy
> - has power

The Bible claims to be a revelation from God. Revelation refers to the content of Scripture, which originated with God and not with humans. David said about the source of the content of his speaking,

> "The Spirit of the Lord spoke through me,
>   his word was on my tongue" (2 Sam. 23:2).

Jeremiah spoke of the source of his message in this manner: "Then the Lord reached out his hand and touched my mouth and said to me, 'Now, I have put my words in your mouth' " (1:9).

The New Testament presents the same emphasis. For example, in 1 Corinthians 7 Paul discussed several issues about sexual purity and marriage. Some of his teaching was based on Jesus' teaching during His earthly ministry, but about a believer's marriage to an unbeliever he had no direct saying of Jesus. Instead, he said: "To the rest I say this (I, not the Lord)" (v. 12). This does not mean that we can ignore this as Paul's opinion. Rather, Paul placed his teaching on the same level with that of the Lord because the content of both came from God. This interpretation is confirmed clearly in 1 Corinthians 14:37: "If anybody thinks he is a prophet or spiritually gifted, let him acknowledge that what I am writing to you is the Lord's command." In Acts 4:25 Luke expressed his conviction that the Holy Spirit spoke through David; that is, the Spirit revealed the content to David. Peter placed Paul's writings on the same level as other Scriptures, meaning the Old Testament: "His [Paul's] letters contain some things that are hard to understand, which ignorant and unstable people distort, as they do the other Scriptures, to their own destruction" (2 Pet. 3:16).

▼THINK ABOUT IT

Circle the word or the phrase that best completes each sentence.

1. Paul placed his teaching on the same level as that of (the Lord, the other apostles).
2. Peter (did, did not) recognize Paul's writings as Scripture.

Paul considered his teaching on the same level as that of the Lord. Peter believed that Paul's content came from the same source as that of the Old Testament authors.

The Bible claims to be inspired. The word *inspiration* means

God-breathed. Inspiration refers to the transmission of content from God to humanity through persons. Paul wrote, "All Scripture is God-breathed" (2 Tim. 3:16). The actual words of Scripture are inspired and are God's words. That is what Peter wrote in 2 Peter 1:21: "Prophecy never had its origin in the will of man, but men spoke from God as they were carried along by the Holy Spirit."

The writers of Scripture "spoke from God." "Carried along by the Holy Spirit" points to inspiration, and "spoke from God" refers to revelation. God used human instruments, but the text makes clear that their writing was not an act of human initiative. The Bible is not a record of humanity's attempt to find or explain God but God's revelation of Himself. God did not destroy the personality of the human instruments but rather guided, controlled, and protected them from error, so much so that Peter could write that they spoke from God. Since they were human authors, they wrote in normal language, using figures of speech and illustrations common to their times and geographical locations. Russ Bush calls inspiration "a personal relationship between the Holy Spirit and the biblical writer." It was a "spiritually-guided process of writing out the message God wanted communicated to His people through the Bible."[9]

THINK ABOUT IT

Circle the word or the phrase that best completes each sentence.

1. God inspired (Scripture, the writers of Scripture) to produce the Bible.
2. God (used, ignored) human personalities in producing Scripture.

God inspired the Scripture itself, and He used human personalities in its writing.

The Bible claims to be trustworthy. We must now address
another question: Did God reveal Himself in a trustworthy and
accurate way? This question introduces the terms *inerrancy* and
infallibility. Common usage makes little distinction between the
two terms. In classical usage *infallibility* signifies the full
trustworthiness of a guide that is not deceived and does not
deceive. *Inerrancy* speaks of "the total truthfulness of a source of
information that contains no mistakes."[10] *Inerrancy* means that
"the Bible, properly understood (in light of its ancient cultural
form and content), is absolutely truthful in all of its affirmations
about God's will and God's way."[11] What Scripture says, God says.
All of it is true.

Answering two questions will help in this discussion.

1. If God desired to reveal Himself to humanity, would He reveal
   Himself in a totally accurate (inerrant) and reliable (infallible)
   way? We must of necessity answer yes, for God is not deceitful
   or capricious. He is truthful and perfect. Such a God would
   certainly make Himself known in a way that is consistent with
   His perfect nature.

2. Would God protect and preserve a written record of His
   revelation of Himself to humankind? Some argue that we
   cannot have an inerrant text, because God used humans to
   write Scripture. If we accept the premise that God is not
   capricious and would desire to protect and preserve a perfect
   revelation, then we are left with only one option if we answer
   that the text contains errors. That option is that He desired to
   protect His Word but was unable to do so. This leaves us in the
   untenable position of believing that God is limited in what He
   is able to do. Could not the God who created the world, who
   came to earth in human flesh, who raised Christ Jesus from the
   grave also protect His written revelation from error? If we agree
   that He would desire to give us a perfect record and that He
   could protect His Word, we are left with the historical position

of evangelical Christianity: the Bible is an inerrant record of God's revelation of Himself.

Thus, we are able to come from a position of strength when we speak on issues of life and eternity. When inerrancy is rejected, we become less sure of Scripture's authority, less certain of our own faith, and more susceptible to alternative views. An errant text would demand an inerrant interpreter to show us the errors so we would not build our worldview on error. Such a view would force the reader to depend on a theological expert to warn him of suspect passages.

THINK ABOUT IT

Circle the word or the phrase that best completes each sentence.

1. The concepts of the inerrancy and infallibility of Scripture (are very similar, contradict each other).
2. Scripture can be trusted in (all, spiritual) matters it addresses.

The concepts of inerrancy and infallibility are similar, referring to the Bible's accuracy and reliability, respectively. Scripture can be trusted in all matters it addresses.

The Bible claims to have power because of its divine origin and purpose. We might read a great classic and be moved to tears or even inspired, but no other book has had as great an impact on humankind through the centuries as the Bible. Read the Bible's claims about its power.

> I am not ashamed of the gospel, because it is the power of God for the salvation of everyone who believes: first for the Jew, then for the Gentile (Rom. 1:16).

> All Scripture is God-breathed and is useful for
> teaching, rebuking, correcting and training in
> righteousness, so that the man of God may be
> thoroughly equipped for every good work (2 Tim.
> 3:16-17).

> The word of God is living and active. Sharper than
> any double-edged sword, it penetrates even to
> dividing soul and spirit, joints and marrow; it
> judges the thoughts and attitudes of the heart
> (Heb. 4:12).

Each case depicts the Word itself as powerful. The Word penetrates soul and spirit, judging our thoughts and intents. The truth of the Word has the power to save, and Scripture is profitable for Christian training. Most Christians could give personal testimonies about the Word's impact in their lives, relating incidents when the Word alone brought conviction and transformation.

▼THINK ABOUT IT

Each of the following statements is false. Rewrite the italicized portion to make each one true.

1. Revelation is *Christians' attempt to discover God.*

   _____

   _____

   _____

2. Inspiration is the process of *creative men's writing holy words from God.*

   _____

---

3. Inerrancy means that the Bible is without error *only in spiritual matters.*

---

4. The Bible has power *only for those who acknowledge its authority.*

WHAT ABOUT BIBLE DIFFICULTIES?

Sometimes Christians are confronted with the question "How can you believe the Bible when it has so many errors and inconsistencies?" Many such objections arise from immaterial or uninformed impressions. Most result from an exposure to negative attitudes about the Bible rather than a firsthand investigation of its contents.

Common objections such as the dates in the Old Testament or the two accounts of the creation in Genesis 1—2 can be answered with relative ease. *The Encyclopedia of Bible Difficulties* by Gleason L. Archer is a reliable source of information written especially to solve Bible difficulties.

Another argument suggests that the early church distorted the

Gospels, rewriting them and supplementing them to create its own story. First, the time between A.D. 47 and 70 was not sufficient for that to occur. Second, the eyewitnesses, both inside and outside the Christian movement, would have immediately cried foul. Further, it is difficult to believe that so great a number of people joyfully gave their lives for what they knew to be a manufactured story.

Some critics of Scripture offer simply a vague objection to historical accuracy. That charge has been thoroughly discredited by archaeological information in the 20th century. The charges of historical blunder are easy to refute because the authors of Scripture made numerous references to historical events that could have been easily checked by contemporaries of their own day. For example, in Luke 1:1-5 Luke indicated his desire for his readers to know the exact truth. He then mentioned the king of Judea. Throughout his two-volume work, Luke and Acts, he continually made historical references. If Luke had made numerous incredible historical blunders, they would have been obvious to any contemporary reader and would have immediately discredited his writings.

Suppose I began a message with the statement "This is the exact truth" but then referred to an event that occurred in 1992, the year Jimmy Carter was president. Would you give serious attention to my message? Of course not. You would rightly think, *Why should I listen to anyone who is so out of touch with reality?* It is amazing that persons today think that they can spot historical errors in the Bible that went unnoticed by contemporaries of the biblical authors. And many of those contemporaries would have had reason to discredit the Gospel writers and to destroy the Christian movement.

Some argue that the Bible does not claim that it is inerrant. It is true that the word *inerrant* does not occur in Scripture; but neither does the word *Trinity*, an idea that is clearly taught. Any fair reading of the New Testament would convince us that Jesus regarded the Scriptures as inerrant. When He referred to Old Testament events or people, He referred to them as historically accurate events. On numerous occasions He referred to the Word of God as absolutely authoritative. Look for the obvious meanings in the following passages.

> "Do not think that I have come to abolish the Law or the Prophets; I have not come to abolish them but to fulfill them. I tell you the truth, until heaven and earth disappear, not the smallest letter, not the least stroke of a pen, will by any means disappear from the Law until everything is accomplished" (Matt. 5:17-18).

> "Heaven and earth will pass away, but my words will never pass away" (Mark 13:31).

> "It is easier for heaven and earth to disappear than for the least stroke of a pen to drop out of the Law" (Luke 16:17).

On one occasion Jesus had been accused of blasphemy. In defending Himself, He referred only to the Scriptures and declared, " 'The Scripture cannot be broken' " (John 10:35). He never "corrected" the text of Scripture. He always assumed it to be truthful and taught people how His ministry fulfilled it. It is inconsistent for those who accept Jesus as Lord to reject His view of Scripture. In an attempt to avoid this obvious dilemma, some argue that Jesus either accommodated Himself to the prejudices of His contemporaries or was limited by His culture. This suggestion creates incredible problems because Jesus' view of Scripture was at the heart of His teaching. Can we believe in Jesus for salvation and at the same time think that He based His teaching on a view of Scripture that was wrong? Nothing in the New Testament suggests that Jesus accommodated Himself in other areas. Why would He accommodate Himself in this critical area?

Some objections to inerrancy are based on the use of figures of speech or symbolic numbers. Laughingly, the critic asks: "You believe the Bible is literally true; then what kind of door is Jesus?" (see John 10:9). "Do you really believe that the trees in the fields clapped their hands?" (see Isa. 55:12). Such suggestions are ludicrous. Figures of speech do not constitute errors in biblical speech any more than in modern speech. The context is always a sufficient guide to interpret such references. A belief in inerrancy does not mean a wooden, literal interpretation of the text.

THINK ABOUT IT
How would you answer the cartoon character's question?

How can we know that the Bible is true and not just filled with myths and stories?

WHAT ARE EVIDENCES OF THE BIBLE'S UNIQUENESS?
We have already noted that mathematically, we cannot prove an axiom. Nevertheless, an axiom proves itself over time as it is

applied repeatedly and is found true in situation after situation. The evidence points to the accuracy of our conclusion that God has spoken and that He has provided humanity with an accurate record of His message to us, which we call the Bible. What, then, is the evidence?

Reliability of the biblical documents. Both the quantity and the quality of the manuscripts of the Scripture should give us confidence in the Bible's accuracy. In the case of the Old Testament, the Hebrew texts are unusually well preserved. They have proved themselves to be exceptionally reliable and have been supported by the Dead Sea Scrolls. Therefore, we need not doubt the Old Testament's reliability.

With over 5,000 Greek manuscripts and 8,000 Latin manuscripts, no other book in ancient literature can compare with the New Testament in documentary support. We have 7 ancient copies of Plato's writings, 5 of Aristotle's, and 643 of Homer's. Moreover, the quality of the various New Testament manuscripts is without parallel in the ancient world. Because of the great reverence the Jewish scribes and early Christians had for the Scriptures, they exercised extreme care in accurately copying and preserving the authentic text. Because we have thousands of manuscripts, readings may vary in places; but these usually resulted from visual or auditory errors in the copying process. Most relate to spellings. Only a minute number would affect the understanding of the text. None call into question a major doctrine or factual teaching. The reliability of the manuscripts points to the Bible's uniqueness.

Historical accuracy of the Bible. We have already referred to the historical reliability of the Bible. Numerous detailed references to historical events throughout the Bible give ample opportunity to examine the claim of historical accuracy.

During the early 19th century the science of archaeology began to flourish. Archaeologists dig under the earth to examine the remains of the past, and their findings have often revealed places and names from the Old Testament. Many thought that the findings of archaeologists would destroy faith in the historicity of the Bible. But the opposite effect has resulted. Archaeology has confirmed the Bible's historical and geographic accuracy. For example, W. F. Albright, late professor emeritus of Johns Hopkins University, remarked, "Until recently it was the fashion among biblical historians to treat the patriarchal sagas of Genesis as though they were artificial creations of Israelite scribes of the Divided Monarchy or tales told by imaginative rhapsodists around Israelite campfires."[12] Albright concluded, "There can be no doubt that archaeology has confirmed the substantial historicity of Old Testament tradition."[13]

Sir William Ramsay was a wealthy atheist with a doctorate in philosophy from Oxford University. He gave his entire life to archaeology in order to disprove the Bible. After 25 years of work he became particularly impressed with the historical accuracy of Luke and Acts, then shocked the world by declaring himself to be a Christian.

Fulfilled prophecy. The Scriptures are filled with predictive prophecies. Some three hundred Old Testament prophecies were fulfilled in the life of Christ. These prophecies are so minutely accurate that some have suggested that Jesus attempted to engineer His life to fulfill messianic prophecies. This is an untenable suggestion since many prophecies relate to His birth, death, and resurrection, events that could not be engineered.

Some have argued that these Old Testament prophecies did not actually point to Christ but that the early church simply interpreted them this way after the fact. Once again, consider Jesus' understanding of prophecy. When Jesus revealed Himself to the men on the road to Emmaus, He rebuked them for not seeing the fulfillment of prophecy in all the events surrounding His death. Then He began to instruct them lovingly; "beginning with

Moses and with all the Prophets, He explained to them what was said in all the Scriptures concerning himself" (Luke 24:27; also see v. 44). The apostle Paul regularly led his Jewish hearers and readers through the Old Testament, explaining and giving evidence that Jesus is the Christ (see Acts 17:2-3).

The Old Testament contains numerous other specific prophecies about events that were fulfilled in the Old Testament period. They are so detailed that they could not be just good guesses. Frequently, the prophet predicted the very opposite of what might be expected to happen.

Impact of the Bible. The Bible was uniquely produced, involving more than 40 authors over a span of more than 1,500 years. These authors included a king, shepherds, a tax collector, a fisherman, and a physician. Their diversity, reflected in their educational levels and socioeconomic life-styles, is evident in their writings. Virtually every known literary form is found in the Bible. Yet "it is a harmonious and continuous message from beginning to end." Most publishers would never dream of inviting 40 different authors with diverse abilities to write on a particular theme and then bind their writings as one continuous book. Yet the Bible is 66 books that form one unified Book. What a powerful testimony to the unique inspiration of the Bible.[14]

No other book can compare with the Bible in terms of sales and influence. It has always been a best-seller. More books are written about the Bible, either to explain it or to explain it away, than any other book in history. It stands at the center of the literary world. It is unique in its endurance. It has been banned and burned and subjected to destructive criticism, and yet it remains. The Bible is unique in its message; it claims to be the very words of Creator God. Finally, the Bible is unique in its power to change a person's life. Throughout the centuries no book can begin to compare with the Bible in its life-changing impact.

Although we may not be able to prove to the skeptic that the

Bible is the Word of God, we can point to the cumulative evidence. We can challenge the skeptics to examine their own prejudices and to read the Bible for themselves.

The sound assurance that God has spoken a sure and reliable Word provides us with a firm foundation on which to build our worldview. We are not left in the realm of speculation when it comes to issues like the origin of life, the problem of evil, human purpose, or our ultimate destiny.

▼HINK ABOUT IT

List the four key evidences of the Bible's uniqueness.

1. _____

2. _____

3. _____

4. _____

AXIOM 4: JESUS CHRIST IS GOD'S SON

What was the first verse of Scripture you memorized? Many would identify John 3:16. As a matter of fact, this verse is quoted so often that it is possible to repeat it without thinking about its meaning.

▼HINK ABOUT IT

Try this experiment. Read John 3:16 but pretend that you have never read this verse before: "God so loved the world, that he gave his only begotten Son, that whosoever believeth in him should not perish, but have everlasting life" (KJV). Now write in your own words what you believe this verse says. Remember that you are pretending to have read John 3:16 for the first time.

Did this most familiar of all Bible verses take on new meaning for you? Many truths could be gleaned from John 3:16, but the primary truth is that God's supreme demonstration of love is that He gave His Son to save us.

We have discussed at length the way God reveals Himself through Scripture. It is important for us to understand that the focal truth of Scripture is that Jesus Christ is the Son of God, whom the Father sent to accomplish our salvation. Everything in the Bible points to this truth: Jesus Christ is the Son of God.

Jesus Christ is the standard of truth by which all beliefs are measured. A good way to distinguish truth from error in religious beliefs is to discover what those beliefs confess about Jesus. Every cult and false doctrine distorts biblical truth about Jesus Christ. Some deny His deity. Others dispute His humanity. Still others try to add human works and efforts to the perfect salvation He has provided.

Several key truths about Jesus are essential to the Christian worldview. Let us take a closer look at these truths.

Jesus is God. This strong statement is fully supported by the teachings of Scripture. Speaking of Jesus, Paul wrote, "He is the image of the invisible God, the firstborn over all creation. For by him all things were created: things in heaven and on earth, visible and invisible, whether thrones or powers or rulers or authorities; all things were created by him and for him. He is before all things, and in him all things hold together "(Col. 1:15-17).

▼THINK ABOUT IT
What does Colossians 1:15-17 teach about Jesus?

Did you include in your answer that this passage teaches that Jesus is God?

Jesus was human. Speaking of Jesus, John 1:1 says: "In the beginning was the Word, and the Word was with God, and the Word was God." As we have already seen, the fact that Jesus is God is beyond dispute. John 1:14 says, "The Word became flesh and made his dwelling among us." This verse emphasizes a very basic truth: the Word (Jesus) became flesh. In other words, He became human. Of course, He never ceased being God. He is God, and He also became human. He was born of Mary without a human father. Mary was a virgin, but she was a human being in every sense of the word. Jesus did not just pretend to be a man. He did not just look like a man. He was not half man and half God. Jesus was born of Mary as a real human being. He lived a perfect, sinless life; but He lived as a real human. He experienced hunger and fatigue. He felt human emotions. He was tempted as a man, but He never sinned: "We do not have a high priest who is unable to sympathize with our weaknesses, but we have one who has been tempted in every way, just as we are—yet was without sin" (Heb. 4:15).

The full deity and humanity of Jesus are truths that are beyond human comprehension, but God is not limited to human reason. The humanity of Jesus must not be ignored, just as His full deity must not be ignored. Biblical faith requires both affirmations.

▼HINK ABOUT IT
What does John 1:1,14 teach about Jesus?

_____

_____

Did you include in your answer that this passage teaches that Jesus was human?

Jesus died on the cross. Few would dispute the historical reality of Jesus' death on the cross. It is the meaning of His death that is important to Christians. Many have died as martyrs to a noble cause, but this does not explain the meaning of Jesus' death. What does it mean? What does it have to do with us today?

Theologians often use the word *substitutionary* to explain the meaning of what Jesus did on the cross. The writer of the Book of Hebrews explained this concept in this powerful passage: "He did not enter by means of the blood of goats and calves; but he entered the Most Holy Place once for all by his own blood, having obtained eternal redemption. For this reason Christ is the mediator of a new covenant, that those who are called may receive the promised eternal inheritance—now that he has died as a ransom to set them free from the sins committed under the first covenant" (Heb. 9:12,15).

His death was a ransom—that is, the price paid for our deliverance from sin's power and penalty. The price He paid was the shedding of His blood. John's words express believers' faith across the centuries: "The blood of Jesus, his Son, purifies us from all sin" (1 John 1:7).

Jesus rose from the grave. Paul summarized the good news of the Christian faith when he wrote to the Corinthians: "What I received I passed on to you as of first importance: that Christ died for our sins according to the Scriptures, that he was buried, that he was raised on the third day according to the Scriptures" (1 Cor. 15:3-4).

The Bible always treats Jesus' resurrection as literal and bodily. Jesus was really dead. He was buried in a tomb. He bodily came out of the tomb. He was seen by many who were willing to testify that they saw Him alive after His death on the cross: "He appeared to Peter, and then to the Twelve. After that, he appeared to more than five hundred of the brothers at the same time, most of whom are still living, though some have fallen asleep. Then he appeared to James, then to all the apostles" (1 Cor. 15:5-7). There is no Christian faith apart from the bodily resurrection of Jesus. Christians do not remember a great, dead leader. We worship and serve a living Lord!

Jesus is Lord. This was the confession of early believers (see Rom. 10:8-10). He is Lord of our individual lives. He is Lord of the church. He is Lord of history. He is Lord of eternity. In one of the most beautiful hymns of praise ever written, Paul wrote:

> God exalted him to the highest place
>   and gave him the name that is above every name,
> that at the name of Jesus every knee should bow,
>   in heaven and on earth and under the earth,
> and every tongue confess that Jesus Christ is Lord,
>   to the glory of God the Father (Phil. 2:9-11).

A recognition of Jesus' lordship is the key to the Christian worldview. All of life is lived under His lordship. The Christian understands that all truth must affirm the supremacy of Christ, that every way of looking at reality must agree with the supreme reality of His lordship. His lordship is both a present reality and a future expectation. Someday He will return to be proclaimed Lord by the entire creation. The believer lives with this truth at the center of life.

THINK ABOUT IT

What is unique about Jesus that qualifies Him to be Lord of all?

_____

_____

_____

Since Jesus is Lord of all, how do you feel about personally submitting to His lordship?

_____

_____

___

[1]Arthur F. Holmes, *Contours of a World View* (Grand Rapids: Eerdmans, 1983), 48.

[2]For a more detailed discussion of these proofs, see Paul Little, *Know Why You Believe* (Downers Grove: InterVarsity, 1968), 23-37, and Norman L. Geisler and Ronald M. Brooks, *When Skeptics Ask* (Wheaton: Victor Books, 1990), 15-33.

[3]Geisler and Brooks, *When Skeptics Ask*, 22.

[4]Fred Hoyle, *The Intelligent Universe* (London: Michael Joseph, 1983), 19.

[5]Charles Darwin, *The Origin of Species* (London: J. M. Denton & Sons, 1942), 167.

[6]Carl Sagan, *Cosmos* (New York: Random House, 1980), 278.

[7]Holmes, *Contours*, 133.

[8]Carl F. H. Henry, *The Christian Mindset in a Secular Society* (Portland: Multnomah, 1984), 34.

[9]L. Russ Bush, *Understanding Biblical Inerrancy* (Fort Worth: Columbia, 1988), 17.

[10]Sinclair B. Ferguson, David F. Wright, and J. I. Packer, eds., *New Dictionary of Theology* (Downers Grove: InterVarsity, 1988), 337.

[11]Bush, *Understanding*, 12. If you are interested in reading more about inerrancy, read L. Russ Bush, *Understanding Biblical Inerrancy*, and James T. Draper, Jr., *Authority: The Critical Issue for Southern Baptists* (New Jersey: Fleming H. Revell, 1984).

[12]William Foxwell Albright, *The Biblical Period from Abraham to Ezra* (New York: Harper and Row, 1963), 1.

[13]Paul Little, *Know Why You Believe* (Downers Grove: InterVarsity, 1968), 49. For more information on the archaeology of the Bible, you would enjoy D. James Kennedy, *Why I Believe* (Dallas: Word, 1980), 27-36; Paul Little, *Know Why You Believe*, 85-99; and Kenneth Boa and Larry Moody, *I'm Glad You Asked* (Wheaton: Victor Books, 1982), 86-90.

[14]Boa and Moody, *I'm Glad You Asked*, 83. For further information about the manuscripts, begin with Boa and Moody, 74-101.

Anthropic principle: The theory that the universe was well tuned for the emergence of life.

Cosmogony: The study of the origin of the universe.

Darwinism: The theory that all species have developed over long periods of time through the processes of mutation and natural selection.

Entropy: The amount of useless or random energy in a controlled system.

Ex nihilo: *From nothing,* referring to the Christian worldview's conclusion that God made the universe from nothing.

First law of thermodynamics: The scientific observation that mass and energy are interchangeable but cannot be created or destroyed.

Law of biogenesis: The scientific observation that life begets life.

Law of causality: The scientific observation that every effect has a prior cause.

Macroevolution: The evolutionary theory that all living things descended from earlier living things, tracing their origins to the primordial soup from which life emerged.

Materialism: The belief that matter is the ultimate reality.

Microevolution: The evolutionary theory that all living things are adapting but only within species.

Second law of thermodynamics: The scientific observation that things left to themselves move from order to disorder.

Theistic evolution: An attempt to reconcile evolution with biblical creation by proposing that God began and continues to direct the process of evolution.

WHAT IS OUR ORIGIN?

"The Cosmos is all that is or ever was or ever will be. . . . Our obligation to survive is owed not just to ourselves but also to that Cosmos, ancient and vast, from which we spring."[1] How do we respond to those statements by Carl Sagan, the well-known author and proponent of evolution? Do we disagree? Strongly or mildly? Why? Does the question of our origin really make any difference? Should we just leave those questions to scientists?

Christians who believe the Bible cannot afford to shrug their shoulders and pretend that these questions do not matter. Those who are truly interested in developing a consistent worldview cannot ignore the issue of origins. The importance of this issue is agreed on by both those who believe in creation and those who argue for evolution. The matter of the beginning of life is a crucial issue for all worldviews. Carl Sagan believes not only that we are created in the image of the cosmos but also that we actually have a duty to perpetuate its existence. Thus, our well-being depends on scientific knowledge, and scientists begin to function as priests who remind us of our ethical obligations and point us to the way of salvation.[2] Likewise, most evangelical confessions of faith either begin with or include a belief in creation. For example, the first line of the Apostles' Creed is "I believe in God the Father Almighty, Maker of heaven and earth."[3]

WHAT IS AT STAKE?

Why is the matter of origins so critical? We will look at that question in this chapter, but first let us consider a few implications of creation and evolution. If we are created in the image of God, then human life is sacred and has special value. If, on the other hand, we evolved by chance, then human life has no greater significance than animal life or plant life. This foundational understanding would affect our thinking on matters such as the value of the elderly, the handicapped, the terminally ill, or the unborn.

▼HINK ABOUT IT

Record statements about the value of life you have recently read or heard that appear to be influenced by an evolutionary worldview.

_____

_____

_____

_____

If we are the product of a Creator, then we have a moral obligation to serve and obey Him. If our Creator has established moral laws, then they are absolutes. Secular humanists recognize this implication of creation. They clearly see that if no God exists, no basis for moral absolutes exists. In their *Humanist Manifesto* they conclude: "Moral values derive their source from human experience. Ethics is *autonomous* and *situational,* needing no theological or ideological sanction. Ethics stems from human need and interest."[4] Thus, their conclusion about the beginning of life leads them to accept the right to abortion, euthanasia, and any form of sexual behavior between consenting adults.

Our belief about the beginning of life definitely affects our values. The conclusion that humankind is the work of a sovereign Creator means that we must follow His prescription for living if we are to enjoy life. I am convinced that many Christians who do not accept the evolutionary premise of beginnings have unwittingly accepted many of the moral conclusions that emerge from such thinking. I often hear Christians say, "I know that homosexuality is wrong for me, but who am I to judge the lifestyle of another?" or "Perhaps abortion is the most loving alternative in some situations." Do you see the subjective nature of such thinking? It is based on the premise that no absolutes exist.

EVOLUTION VERSUS CREATION

EVOLUTION *Humans are the center.*	**CREATION** *God is the center.*
• No Creator; chance	• Creator; purpose
• Humans evolved by time and chance	• Humans were made in God's image (Gen. 1:26)
• Humans are the product of the survival of the fittest	• Humans are wonderfully made by design (Ps. 139:13-14)
• No absolutes; situation ethics; homosexuality, adultery, racism, abortion	• God's Word is truth (Ps. 119:160), containing absolutes about all issues of life
• No moral obligation	• Humans are obligated to the Creator (Rom. 8:12-13)
• Human life has same value as animal and plant life	• Human life has greater value than animal and plant life (Gen. 1:28)
• Humans serve and satisfy self	• Humans serve the Creator, not His creation (Rom. 1:25)
↓	↓
Secular Humanism	*Biblical Theism*

▼HINK ABOUT IT

For Christians the issue of origins is critical for another reason. It
is the foundation for many basic Christian doctrines. Read the
following verses and match each creation narrative with the related
teaching.

___ 1.	Psalm 24:1-4	a.	Marital relationship
___ 2.	Matthew 19:4-6	b.	Salvation
___ 3.	Romans 5:12,17	c.	Christ's second coming
___ 4.	1 Corinthians 15:45-49	d.	Purity
___ 5.	Colossians 1:12-16	e.	Forgiveness of sin
___ 6.	2 Peter 3:3-11	f.	Resurrection body

Answers: 1. d, 2. a, 3. b, 4. f, 5. e, 6. c.

Did you notice that doctrines such as sin and salvation, the
resurrection of the believer, and the second coming are specifically
related to the creation narrative? Other matters, such as marriage
and authority in the home or the church, are also tied to the
Genesis account of creation.

Much is at stake in our study of the question, What is our
origin? Therefore, we cannot afford to pretend that it does not
matter what we believe about the origin of life.

WHAT ARE THE OPTIONS?

How did we come to exist? Hold it! I am not asking for a birth
certificate and a short lecture about the birds and the bees. I am
asking a more fundamental question about our origin.

Basically, we have three options for answering the question of
our existence: we are self-caused, uncaused, or caused by another.
We do not need to say much about self-caused, for it is clearly
impossible to have brought ourselves into existence. If we argue

that we are uncaused, we confront an obvious contradiction. If we are uncaused beings, then we are by necessity eternal, infinite beings. Overwhelming evidence proves that this is not the case. Therefore, we must be caused.

This leads us to the obvious question about the ultimate cause of life: What process or being is responsible for the creation of life, specifically human existence? Normally, a created object gives us fairly accurate clues about the creator. For example, we can look at a painting and draw conclusions about the artist's skill. When we look at a complex office building and compare it to a primitive mud hut, we come to certain conclusions about the designer and builder of each. If we objectively looked at our complex and uniquely balanced world, we would conclude that an intelligent Designer is at work. If we look at humans, we might further surmise that the Creator is personal, intelligent, and moral. But we are jumping ahead of ourselves. In fairness we must examine alternative views of life's origin. We can consider only four alternatives.

The universe is an illusion. This self-defeating idea can be discarded. If the universe truly is an illusion, then this book is also an illusion, as is its reader. This suggestion lacks rational coherence and factual correspondence. To believe this, we would have to reject all the evidence apprehended through our five senses. Our personal relationships establish illusionism as a lie. Even the most hardened skeptic would refuse to step in front of a truck, claiming it to be only an illusion.

The universe is eternal. In this case the universe would be uncaused and, in some inexplicable way, would account for its own existence. Many scientists have favored this position until recently. First, it enables its proponent to avoid the obvious question of who caused the universe. Second, it provides the infinite time that would be required if all complex life forms emerged from nonliving matter. Many scientists have relied on infinite time plus chance to explain the origin of life. Yet the difficulties of this proposition have caused those same scientists to point out its weakness. Fred Hoyle used this analogy to illustrate the difficulties: How long would it take a blindfolded person to solve a Rubik's Cube? If he made one move per second, without resting, it would take an astonishing 1,350 billion years. Hoyle then explained that it would be equally difficult for the accidental formation of only one of the many chains of amino acids needed to make one human cell. It would take about 293.5 times the estimated age of the earth, set at the standard 4.5 billion years.[5]

In *I'm Glad You Asked* Boa and Moody present several scientific observations that make this position untenable.[6]

1. It violates a fundamental law of science, the law of causality, which states that every effect has a prior cause. If this law is not consistent, then science cannot function. To believe in an eternal universe requires believing that events happened without a cause. Even the great skeptic David Hume said, "I never asserted so absurd a proposition as that anything might arise without a cause."[7]

2. The evidence of cosmogony, that is, the study of the origin of the universe, rules against an eternal universe. Edwin Hubble's discovery that the universe is uniformly expanding in all directions led George Gamov to suggest that if we reversed the process, tracing the expanding universe into the distant past, we would reach the point when all matter was compressed into a dense, hot primordial atom. Gamov's big-bang theory holds that the atom exploded immediately after creation. While we need not accept all of Gamov's hypothesis, this evidence from cosmogony is important because it asserts that the universe had a definite point of beginning. Thus, it is finite and not infinite.

3. The presence of an abundance of hydrogen in the universe argues against this view. Throughout the universe hydrogen is converted into helium through the process of nuclear fusion in

the cores of the stars. This process is irreversible, and new hydrogen is not formed in any significant amounts by the breakdown of heavier atoms. Therefore, if the universe were infinitely old, we would expect that there should be almost no hydrogen left. Yet most of the universe is made up of hydrogen.

4. The second law of thermodynamics suggests that the universe had a beginning. The first law of thermodynamics, the law of the conservation of mass and energy, states that mass and energy are interchangeable but cannot be created or destroyed. The second law states that the quality of energy in the universe is constantly declining. *Entropy* refers to the amount of useless or random energy in any closed system. The energy does not disappear, but it simply cannot be reorganized to perform work. As time increases, entropy increases, and the universe itself will eventually burn out. This process indicates that the universe is finite.

The astrophysicist Robert Jastrow concluded that "three lines of evidence—the motions of the galaxies, the laws of thermodynamics, and the life story of the stars—pointed to one conclusion; all indicated that the Universe had a beginning."[8] Hugh Ross, an imminent astronomer, in his book *The Fingerprint of God* deals with the various theories of the organization of the universe. He concludes: "With the defeat of the static, hesitation, steady state, and oscillation models for the universe, no observationally testable alternative remained (by 1984) to make the universe infinitely old and thereby to save evolutionism."[9]

The universe emerged from nothing. This position clearly conflicts with the law of causality. All reason and observation confirm that nothing cannot produce something. When applied to the issue of life itself, it contradicts the law of biogenesis, which states that life begets life. No one would seriously think that a VCR simply came into being without a cause. Yet many scientists are left with this untenable position in their attempts to defend evolutionism and to avoid the conclusion of a created universe.

The universe was created by an eternal Being. This is the only remaining option if we conclude that the universe is real, finite, and caused. You will immediately recognize that this is precisely the argument of the theistic worldview. The Christian worldview, based on the creation of the universe from nothing (*ex nihilo*), best answers the question of the origin of life.[10]

▼HINK ABOUT IT

List the four theories of the origin of life and describe each in your own words.

1. _____

_____

2. _____

_____

3. _____

_____

4. _____

_____

Which theory is most prevalent in society?

_____

How Does the Question of Origins Relate to Our Worldview?

A worldview's perspective on the issue of origins affects its entire system of thought. Various worldviews begin from radically different perspectives on this issue. We will examine three ways of looking at origins and the belief systems that undergird these views.

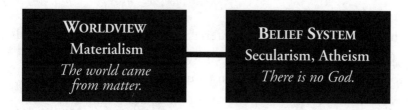

Worldview
Materialism
The world came from matter.

Belief System
Secularism, Atheism
There is no God.

Materialism

Materialism, the belief that matter is ultimate reality, follows an evolutionary model of origins. The materialist believes that it is unnecessary to assert God's existence in order to explain the universe. For the materialist, matter simply exists; and ultimately, everything, including mind, evolved from preexisting matter. Karl Marx succinctly stated this view: "Matter is not a product of mind, but mind itself is merely the highest product of matter."[11] Atheism is the logical outcome of strict materialism. As the *Humanist Manifesto II* puts it, "As non-theists, we begin with humans not God, nature not deity."[12]

The implications of this system of thought are profound. Humanity, though accorded the highest position on the evolutionary ladder, is not qualitatively different from animals. The strict materialist believes that persons are not spiritual beings. In fact, the strict materialist does not believe in spirit or mind. There is no mind, only a brain that produces thought through chemical processes. As we will note in the next chapter, the moral values that have issued from the evolutionary worldview have had catastrophic effects on society.

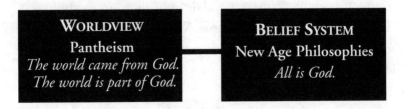

| WORLDVIEW Pantheism *The world came from God. The world is part of God.* | BELIEF SYSTEM New Age Philosophies *All is God.* |

Pantheism

This view is the opposite of materialism. Pantheists believe that all is God. They do not believe in creation apart from God. The world is an evolving cosmic consciousness of which humans are insignificant parts. We are all part of God, and we must be awakened to that reality. Absolute pantheists deny the existence of matter; it is an illusion. Others believe that matter emanates from God. When applied to creation, this belief means that there is a Creator but no creation. All creatures are part of the Creator. They come from Him the way a flower unfolds from a seed. Creatures are simply many drops that splash up from the infinite pond, only to drop back in eventually and blend with the rest. Thus, God and the world are of the same substance. God is water and trees. If this sounds like New Age rhetoric, it is. One New Age writer said, "While watching his little sister drink her milk, 'All of a sudden I saw that she was God and the *milk* was God. I mean, all she was doing was pouring God into God.' "[13]

Since pantheists assert that God and the creation are of the same essence, then the creation must be both eternal and infinite. Thus, all the arguments that refute the beliefs of evolutionists, who believe that the universe is eternal, also apply to pantheists. If the universe had a beginning and God did not, then this system fails to deal with observable scientific facts. Further, if we come from God, who is by definition unchanging, and yet we can observe readily that we are changing, then we cannot be of the same substance as God. The play may come from the playwright or the painting from the painter; but the play is not part of the playwright, nor is the painting part of the painter. The creation is a separate entity from the Creator.

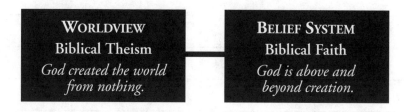

WORLDVIEW
Biblical Theism
God created the world from nothing.

BELIEF SYSTEM
Biblical Faith
God is above and beyond creation.

Biblical Theism

According to this view, God created everything from nothing. God is above and beyond the world. He is not contained within the world, but He stands solely as its author. Many other religious systems see the gods as part of creation. The Mesopotamian gods were identified with celestial bodies. Some primitive beliefs deify animals. But the biblical view holds that God alone is divine, that the heavens declare the glory of God, bearing sufficient witness to Him.

Consider Paul's words about creation in Romans 1:20-21: "Since the creation of the world God's invisible qualities—his eternal power and divine nature—have been clearly seen, being understood from what has been made, so that men are without excuse. For although they knew God, they neither glorified him as God nor gave thanks to him, but their thinking became futile and their foolish hearts were darkened." When persons refused to worship God and began to worship the creation, they became morally confused and society decayed, as the remainder of Romans 1 clearly indicates. The implications of creation from nothing are profound, forming the basic framework for biblical Christianity.

▼HINK ABOUT IT

How will your views about the origin of the world affect your life-style?

_____

_____

_____

_____

_____

_____

WHAT ABOUT EVOLUTION?

Despite the recent growth of the pantheistic worldview, accelerated by the popularity of New Age thinking, most Christians struggle more with the question of evolution versus creation. In part, this is true because of the predominance of the evolutionary viewpoint in our school systems. Most people have been educated to believe that evolution is fact and that all scientists believe in evolution. This impression may intimidate the average person who does not claim scientific expertise.

Many Christians have attempted simply to accommodate the evolutionary worldview to their biblical faith, unaware of the conflicts that such accommodation creates. These persons generally hold some form of theistic evolution. They would accept the findings of evolutionists but would argue that God began the process and continues to direct the process. Although this intermediate position, called theistic evolution, may at first sound plausible, it is impossible to maintain.

Russ Bush points out several flaws in this view of origins. First,

urged against the theory. The explanation lies, as I believe, in the extreme imperfection of the geological record."[18] The passing of years has not improved the evidence for creation from the geological record. New species suddenly appear in the fossil record without any transitional sequences—not what one would expect if evolution answered the question of the origin of life.

Evolution does not adequately answer the question of origins. To maintain the belief in evolution, one must ignore many proven laws of science. In fact, the evidence from science suggests a finite universe, the origin and development of which can best be accounted for by an intelligent Creator. Some scientists have pointed to the unique design and habitability of the universe as evidence of a Creator. The anthropic principle has recently gained great attention. According to this principle, the universe was well tuned for the emergence of human life. Commenting on this, one agnostic scientist confessed, "The anthropic principle is the most interesting development next to the proof of the creation, and it is even *more* interesting because it seems to say that science itself has proven, as a hard fact, that this universe was made, was designed, for man to live in. It's a very theistic result."[19]

THINK ABOUT IT

Mark the following statements *T* for true or *F* for false, based on the information in the preceding section.

___ 1. *Nothing + time = life* is an accepted scientific axiom.
___ 2. Scientists have proved that unique conditions for the origin of life once existed but no longer exist.
___ 3. Mutation and natural selection do not create new life forms.
___ 4. Mathematical probability demonstrates that life resulted from a chance act of evolution.

___ 5. The geological discoveries of the past century do not
       support the theory of evolution.

Answers: 1. F, 2. F, 3. T, 4. F, 5. T.

A Critical Question

If all the scientific evidence bases the origin of life in a Creator,
then why do so many scientists still believe in evolution? Perhaps
that question is best answered by the scientists themselves. The
famous British evolutionist Sir Arthur Keith said, "Evolution is
unproved and unprovable. We believe it because the only
alternative is special creation which is unthinkable."[20] D. M. S.
Watson observed that evolution is a theory universally acceptable
"not because it has been observed to occur or can be proved by
logically coherent evidence to be true, but because the only
alternative—special creation—is clearly incredible."[21] L. H.
Matthew, in his foreword to a new edition of Darwin's *Origin of
Species,* wrote, "Belief in evolution is . . . exactly parallel to belief in
special creation—both are concepts which believers *know to be
true,* but neither, up to the present, has been capable of proof."[22]
Robert T. Clark and James D. Bales, in *Why Scientists Accept
Evolution*, cite letters from Charles Darwin, Thomas Huxley,
Herbert Spencer, and other early evolutionists who acknowledged
that their hostility toward God and their bias against the
supernatural had caused them to embrace evolution. Henry M.
Morris has pointed out that an evolutionary view of humans as
animals also makes it convenient for persons to release sexual
inhibitions and gratify sexual desires without regard for the
consequences.[23]

As you can clearly see, the belief in evolution is precisely that—
a belief system. It is based on faith presuppositions and actually
contradicts many scientific principles. For some, evolution has

become a surrogate religion that replaces the need for God. Some scientists hold tenaciously to evolution precisely because they do not want to believe in God. They reject the notion of God because He cannot be examined in a laboratory for proof. Some scientists accurately understand that recognizing God's existence has implications for how we live. Humanists openly acknowledge that evolutionism is the foundation for their whole belief system.

▼HINK ABOUT IT
The author states that evolution is a belief system based on faith presuppositions. Underline the statements in the previous section that support this assertion.

WHAT IS THE BIBLICAL VIEW OF ORIGINS?
What does the Bible teach about the origin of the world, and what does its teaching mean? It is possible to get so tied up in secondary issues that we miss the primary ones. The Genesis account is less concerned with the questions of how and when than with who and why. While the Genesis account contains reliable scientific affirmations, its focus is on theology rather than on geology or biology. What, then, is the biblical view of origins?

God alone is the infinite Creator. He is the uncaused Cause. Genesis 1:1 begins with the affirmation "In the beginning God." Out of nothing God brought forth everything that exists. The writer of Hebrews stated this same truth: "By faith we understand that the universe was formed at God's command, so that what is seen was not made out of what was visible" (Heb. 11:3). The initial simple but profound statement "In the beginning God created" stands against all false religions. It affirms monotheism against all forms of polytheism; the Bible affirms that there is only one God. Although He is the Creator of the universe, He is not to be identified with His creation, nor is He contained by any region of nature. These facts would rule out any pantheistic view of the world and the use of magic or astrology.

God is not dependent on anything, but all things are dependent on Him. God does not require the creation to make Him complete. He was complete in Himself before creation, but He created the world from love and with purpose. Because God requires nothing outside Himself, we can know that He freely chose whether to create and what to create. Thus, we exist by divine purpose.

THINK **A**BOUT **I**T

Complete this sentence: God alone is the _____
_____.

God said that creation is good. In the Genesis account the repeated phrase "it was good" indicates that each creative act was exactly what God had purposed. Every event of creation corresponded to His eternal purpose and therefore was given appropriate value by its Creator, who pronounced it to be good. Creation does not possess divinity, as pantheism and some evolutionary views claim, but it has dignity and value because it was created with purpose for the habitation of man and woman, who were created in God's image. This truth provides the objective basis for ecological concerns, in addition to the creation's aesthetic and economic value.

THINK **A**BOUT **I**T

Complete this sentence: God said that creation is _____.

God created humans, male and female, in His image. We read so much in our day about the importance of a positive self-image. Nothing could be as affirming as the biblical account of creation. The sovereign God of the universe created you in His image to rule over all creation. Little value can be attached to the view of human life that suggests that persons are merely the products of chance mutation and natural selection, a higher order of the animal kingdom.

We are told in Genesis 1:24-25 that the animals were made after their kind. While this statement certainly notes the uniqueness of each kind of animal, it primarily emphasizes the contrast between animals and humans. Animals are created after their own kind, but humans (vv. 26-27) are created in the image and likeness of God. Humans are not higher animals but unique creations of God, made in His own likeness. Only humans have body, soul, and spirit. Humans' physical attributes may organically and functionally be like those of many animals, but humans are more than physical beings. They have the unique capacity to think, to feel emotion, to choose, and to communicate. We do not find all of these capacities in any developed form, even in higher animals.

Yet even beyond this dimension humans are spiritual beings. A testimony to this fact is the existence of religious relics and altars dating back between 8,000 and 24,000 years. And the evidence suggests that whenever and wherever we encounter humans, we discover the evidence of their spiritual dimension. Men and women were created in God's image as spiritual beings. This means that humans were created for relationships with their Creator. By creation persons are relational beings. They desire relationships with others. For Adam God created a wife who was fully compatible with him. But even this relationship is secondary to a person's created need to live in relationship with His Creator. Thus, we can understand the often-quoted remark: "In every man's heart there is a God-shaped vacuum."

Think About It

Complete this sentence: God created humans in _____ _____.

God continues to care for His creation. Genesis 2:5-6 mentions cultivating and watering the ground. These verses express God's intention of continual involvement with and care for His creation. God established the natural laws so nature would be sustained with continuity, regularity, and predictability. Because He delegates power to His creation, it is ordered, structured, and governed by law (see Gen. 1:14; Ps. 74:16-17). This understanding of the orderly creation led to the beginning of modern science. Men like Bacon, Galileo, Copernicus, Kepler, Kelvin, Newton, and others believed in a Creator who created the universe and then operated it through natural laws.

In creating humans, God gave them the assignment to work with Him in ruling over and replenishing the earth. Thus, persons are given unique dignity and purpose in working with God in the created order. For this reason God continually imparts existence to His creatures by sustaining them and giving them strength. Isaiah 40:28-31 includes this same emphasis. The name Immanuel, "God with us," speaks of God's continual care for His creation. Because of His great love for humanity, He came to live among us through the incarnation. God entered His creation by giving His Son, who was born of a woman.

▼HINK ABOUT IT

Complete this sentence: God continues to care for _____
_____.

God alone gives reality. God creates outside Himself and grants reality to created beings. As creatures, we are finite, dependent on the infinite Creator. Yet God gives us freedom, which must be exercised within the context of His moral absolutes. No finite being can be absolutely free, for by definition a finite being is limited and dependent. "God's delegation of powers implies that he works through means that he has made: physical, psychological, economic, and political—for all these are delegated powers."[24] We are accountable to the Creator in using His divinely granted freedom. We live in a world under the rule of God's laws, and we remain accountable to Him. Humanity's greatest need is to know and cooperate with the laws of God revealed in nature and in the written revelation we call the Bible.

▼HINK ABOUT IT
Now fill in the blanks to complete a paragraph summarizing the biblical view of origins.

God _____ is the infinite Creator. He called all He created _____. The culmination of God's creative work was the creation of man and woman, both of whom He made in His _____. God continues to _____ for His creation. Because of God's creative work and His continuing involvement with His creation, He alone gives ultimate _____.

WHAT ARE THE IMPLICATIONS OF OUR VIEW OF CREATION?

What is the significance of this emphasis on the origin of creation? It is foundational to our understanding of God, ourselves, our relationships, and the whole of creation.

We cannot overstate the significance of the biblical doctrine of creation. The remaining worldview issues will emerge from our understanding of our origin. Let's take a brief look at several implications of Bible teachings about creation.

1. Creation points to God's existence and sovereignty (see Rom. 1:20; 2 Pet. 3:5).
2. Creation means that the created is accountable to the Creator. This tenet becomes the basis for moral values. Adam was given free choice (see Gen. 2:16-17) and was held accountable for his choice.

3. Human dignity is affirmed by the fact that humans, male and female, are created in God's image.

4. Creation affirms that humans are relational beings. This understanding should influence the way we treat other persons and seek forgiveness and reconciliation for broken relationships.

5. The incarnation, when God became flesh and lived among us through His Son, is wholly consistent with the biblical view of creation.

6. Creation gives humans an important role as caretakers of the created world. This places ecological activities in their proper perspective as an issue of stewardship for which we will be held accountable. For a discussion of Christians' responsibility for God's world, see *The Earth Is the Lord's* by Richard D. Land and Louis A. Moore (Broadman Press, 1992).

7. Creation affirms the Creator's providence and care for His creation. He did not simply create the world and leave it to its own devices, but He remains actively involved in sustaining the creation.

8. Creation provides the structure for authority in family, church, and society (see 1 Cor. 11:1-16; 1 Tim. 2:8-15).

9. The believer's bodily resurrection is consistent with the biblical view of the world (see 1 Cor. 15:45-49). Thus, we have a basis for our belief in life after death.

10. The Lord's second coming for judgment and redemption is based on the biblical view of creation (see 2 Pet. 3:3-13).

In the remainder of the study we will consider these implications in greater detail.

¹Carl Sagan, *Cosmos* (New York: Random House, 1980), 4, 345.

²Norman L. Geisler, *Knowing the Truth About Creation* (Michigan: Servant Books, 1989), 114.

³The Apostles' Creed, as quoted by David Bailey Harned, *Creed and Personal Identity* (Philadelphia: Fortress, 1981), 12.

⁴Paul Kurtz, *Humanist Manifestos I & II* (Buffalo: Prometheus, 1973), 17.

⁵Fred Hoyle, *The Intelligent Universe* (London: Michael Joseph, 1983), 11-12, 19-20.

⁶Kenneth Boa and Larry Moody, *I'm Glad You Asked* (Wheaton: Victor Books, 1982), 23-24.

⁷David Hume, *Letters*, ed. J. Y. T. Greig (Oxford: Clarendon, 1932), 1:187, as quoted by Norman L. Geisler and Ronald M. Brooks, *When Skeptics Ask* (Wheaton: Victor Books, 1990), 219.

⁸Geisler, *Knowing the Truth*, 94.

⁹Hugh Ross, *The Fingerprint of God* (Orange, Calif.: Promise, 1991), 107.

¹⁰Boa and Moody, *I'm Glad You Asked*, 22-27.

¹¹Karl Marx, *Marx and Engels on Religion*, ed. Reinhold Niebuhr (New York: Schocken Books, 1964), 231.

¹²Paul Kurtz, *Humanist Manifestos I & II*, 16.

¹³Marilyn Ferguson, *The Aquarian Conspiracy* (Los Angeles: J. P. Tarcher, 1980), 382.

¹⁴L. Russ Bush, *A Handbook for Christian Philosophy* (Grand Rapids: Zondervan, 1991), 122-23.

¹⁵Alan Hayward, *Creation and Evolution* (London: SPCK, 1987), 22.

¹⁶D. James Kennedy, *Why I Believe* (Dallas: Word, 1980), 56.

¹⁷Ibid.

¹⁸Charles Darwin, *The Origin of Species* (New York: E. P. Dutton, 1942), 292-93.

¹⁹Bill Durbin, "A Scientist Caught Between Two Faiths: An Interview with Robert Jastrow," *Christianity Today*, 6 August 1982, 17.

²⁰Kennedy, *Why I Believe*, 51.

²¹Ibid.

²²Hayward, *Creation*, 16.

²³Henry M. Morris, *The Troubled Waters of Evolution* (San Diego: Creation-Life, 1974), 166-68.

²⁴Arthur F. Holmes, *Contours of a World View* (Grand Rapids: Eerdmans, 1983), 64.

Law of diminishing returns: The principle that the more a person has, the more the person needs to be satisfied.

Self-realization: Sometimes called self-actualization; the process of discovering the inner self.

4

WHAT AM I DOING HERE?

Have you ever attended a party or another event and suddenly asked yourself, *What am I doing here?* Perhaps you had little in common with the others present. We all have found ourselves in an awkward situation in which we felt that we did not fit or that we were wasting valuable time.

Let's broaden the field of inquiry: What am I doing here on earth? Why was I born? What am I to do with my life? Will it really matter that I was born or that I occupied space on this planet? Does life have any meaning?

WHY AM I HERE?

This is how a young college student once answered the question, Why am I here? "You're born to be afflicted by your parents throughout your childhood and teenage years. Then you're kicked out of the house to attend a college that you don't want to attend so you can get a well-paying job that you don't like. You spend the rest of your life working and saving so you can finally retire with a little money set aside to enjoy life. But by then you're either too old and tired to enjoy life or you die."

That was not a very positive assessment for a young man who was just turning 20. Certainly, such a view would not stimulate him to try his best in college. It is evident that the answer to the question, Why am I here? will ultimately determine the answer to another question: How should I live?

A clear indication of a generation's philosophy of life is its music. In the turbulent 1960s Peter, Paul, and Mary posed questions of purpose and consistently answered them with the phrase "The answer, my friend, is blowing in the wind," as if to say, "We're not sure why we are here; the answer is blowing in the wind."

Many popular songs of the 1970s and '80s expressed a feeling that life was utter futility. The message implied that life is bad and will not get better. Many of those songs also suggested that the way to deal with the pressures of daily living was to trip out on drugs and forget reality. The idea seemed to be that if people get high enough for long enough, they can ignore the harsh realities of life and create a fantasy world. The purpose of life is pleasure, and we should wring every drop of good times from life before encountering the real world.

A more recent hit song suggested that life's meaning is to be found in the greatest love of all. According to the song, the greatest love is learning to love myself. The real meaning of life is to be found in self-realization or self-actualization. I must look out for *me* and *my* interests and learn to love *myself*.

If music accurately reflects a generation's philosophy and values, we might wonder what the music of the 1990s says about the emerging generation of teenagers and young adults. Groups and singers like Prince, Guns and Roses, Van Halen, Slaughter, and New Kids on the Block tell us that the world stinks. We had better hang on and get our share or, worse yet, drop out. An increasing number of songs advocate suicide at the same time we are confronted with an epidemic of teen suicides. Suicide is now the second highest killer of youth, claiming the lives of 13.5 teens every day. Twenty-seven percent of American teens admit to having thought seriously about suicide. Sixteen percent say that they have planned suicide, and 8 percent have actually attempted suicide. That means that in a one-year period 1,984,160 teens have tried to commit suicide.

Rap music gives frightening insight into the values and mood of our day. Characterized by obscenity, explicit sexual talk, and destructive violence, rap music reflects the anger and despair of many young people, especially in the inner city.

▼**T**HINK ABOUT IT

Can you think of a current song that reflects the way non-Christians view the meaning of life? Write the title of that song. If you recall any lines from the song, write them below also.

_____

_____

_____

_____

_____

_____

How do you think this philosophy of life differs from the Christian perspective?

_____

_____

_____

_____

_____

_____

Has a popular song ever influenced the way you felt about your life? What was that song? How did it influence you?

_____

_____

_____

_____

_____

_____

What is the meaning of life? Why am I here? These questions must be answered because they will ultimately determine our values and the quality of our lives. Those who are unable to give a meaningful answer leave themselves vulnerable to the lures of teen suicide, a drug culture, a host of psychologists and psychiatrists who try to unscramble our confused thinking, and mid-life crisis. Yet few of us have actually given sufficient time and energy to answer the important question, What am I doing here?

What Does the World Offer?

On a continuum of worldviews we have moved from atheism, with its branches of rationalism, to humanism. Humanism is human-centered, having at its foundation an evolutionary view of beginnings. Human beings are here by chance; therefore, the meaning of life is located *in* humans and is determined *by* humans. At the other end of the continuum is biblical theism, which teaches that God created human beings and clearly revealed Himself to them. Life's meaning centers in their relationship with their Creator and is thus determined by Him.

Somewhere in the middle is pantheism, the foundation for much New Age thinking. The purpose-of-life statement in pantheism is often very vague, since we all are God and God is all. The end result of life is to be reabsorbed into the nothingness of the one. Those who hold this view often emphasize the self-realization of human potential, even though one's ultimate goal is to be in harmony with the universe and to be absorbed into nothingness.

These worldviews answer the question, Why am I here? in three different ways.

"Eat, Drink, and Be Merry"

This view, also known as utilitarian individualism, is defined in terms of personal pleasure, happiness, or accumulation. You have heard variations of this philosophy, such as "Go for the gusto" and "You go around only once." The implication is that the meaning of life is determined by the amount of pleasure, power, or things. Recently, I saw a bumper sticker that read, "The one who dies with the most toys wins." This human-centered definition of life is prevalent among humanists and pantheists. If I am the center of the universe, I will find meaning as I satisfy my needs and desires.

A testimony to the powerful influence of utilitarian individualism in our culture is the rapid growth of industries that cater to the wants and desires of modern-day men and women. From luxury vacations to limousine service for youth going to senior proms, we are told to indulge ourselves. After all, we deserve it.

This view of life has an inherent and insurmountable problem: no one has ever accumulated enough to satisfy the longing created by possessions. You would think that a Howard Hughes or a Donald Trump finally would have said, "I have enough." Modern-day athletes are trapped in the spiraling excess of salary negotiations and the possessions those mounting millions can buy, and yet some still confess to a lack of fulfillment. What is the reason? Possessions and pleasure are addictive and thus are governed by the law of diminishing returns. The more a person has, the more he wants.

For example, suppose that a man dreams of owning a boat. The first boat is usually a small ski boat. The owner is thrilled with the new toy and experiences unbridled joy from it until he begins to desire a bigger boat with more power and modern conveniences. Next he buys a 21-foot boat with a more powerful engine. This new toy satisfies for a short period. Then his friends buy large cruisers, and again he becomes dissatisfied. He finds that bigger, more expensive boats provide less gratification. Finally, the boat sits unused on a trailer in the backyard or tied to a dock. Other possessions come to similar ends. Look in your closet or attic to discover the result of utilitarian individualism.

▼THINK ABOUT IT
How has this philosophy influenced you?

_____

_____

_____

_____

_____

_____

"Be All That You Can Be"
This philosophy, called expressive individualism, states that the goal of a person's life is to bring out the creative best, to be all that

she can be. This idea is the foundation of the human-potential and self-realization movements. Pantheists and humanists embrace this belief because they see self as the center of the universe. Through hundreds of self-help and image-enhancement programs and tapes, this prevalent philosophy has influenced many Christians in our society.

The emphasis on loving self and building esteem is healthy and constructive if it is anchored to a biblical view of creation and to responsible community living. If, however, these ideas are not supported by a moral value system, it can breed selfish individualism. Not long ago a brilliant computer engineer divorced his wife of many years and married a woman who, he claimed, encouraged his creativity. His actions were based on the conviction that his highest aim in life was to realize fully his creative potential. Similarly, a successful professional-football coach announced to his wife that their marriage was over, explaining that he no longer had room in his life for both her and his team.

Think About It
How has this philosophy influenced you?

_____

_____

_____

_____

"We Are the World"
According to the philosophy of idealistic altruism, the highest goal in life is to contribute to the good of the whole, as expressed in the song "We Are the World." The lyrics suggest that we are the ones

who can make a better day, so we must start giving. In all fairness, this is a less selfish goal than the two previously discussed.

The problem with this noble idea is consistently living in a way that achieves this goal. Think, for example, about the singers who together recorded "We Are the World." Many of them live a self-centered, pampered life-style marked by excess. Although this goal may seem to be noble, it has appeared to most as unattainably utopian. It does not offer the power needed to overcome human self-centeredness. Alone, it has no power to sustain unselfish living.

THINK ABOUT IT
How has this philosophy influenced you?

_____

_____

_____

_____

The foregoing philosophies offer no long-term, practical answers to the important question, Why am I here? We must look elsewhere for a valid purpose statement for life.

THE BIBLICAL SOLUTION

Does the Christian worldview offer a viable alternative to these views? Indeed, it does! Its purpose statement is balanced and lofty yet practical. Remember that the Christian worldview operates from two axioms: "God is" and "God speaks." Since God is the source of our existence, then our purpose for being must be found in relation to Him. By definition, the created serves the purpose of the Creator.

When we build or design something with our hands, the

primary criterion for evaluating the project's success is the question "Does it suit the purpose for which it was created?" If so, it has meaning and value to the creator. Likewise, we must ask what purpose we were accorded by the Creator. Did the Creator reveal a purpose statement for humans? Because we believe that God spoke in a trustworthy manner, we have a reliable record of His revelation in the Bible. Therefore, we must seek answers in God's Word.

Look again at Genesis, the book of origins. After God completed the creation of the earth and all of its animal inhabitants, He created humans. The creation narrative gives us a clear purpose statement for existence.

> ### GOD'S PURPOSE STATEMENT FOR HUMAN LIFE
> God said, "Let us make man in our image, in our likeness, and let them rule over the fish of the sea and the birds of the air, over the livestock, over all the earth, and over all the creatures that move along the ground."
>
> > So God created man in his own image,
> > in the image of God he created him;
> > male and female he created them.
>
> God blessed them and said to them, "Be fruitful and increase in number; fill the earth and subdue it. Rule over the fish of the sea and the birds of the air and over every living creature that moves on the ground" (Gen. 1:26-28).

All of the animals were created after their own kind; but in contrast, men and women were created in the Creator's image. Being made in God's image means that persons were created as relational beings with the capacity to relate to the Creator and to other created beings. This ability implies responsibility and free will. The purpose statement for both men and women flows from created purpose, providing assurance for *knowing* why we are here. It affirms life, and it gives meaning and purpose to relationships.

As a relational being created in God's image, a person must first relate to the Creator. From this relationship flows responsibility for relationships with other persons and the created order. Consider these truths.

> ### HUMAN BEINGS WERE CREATED . . .
>
> • to have intimate relationships with the Creator
> • for relationships with one another
> • with responsibility for the created order

Human beings were created to have intimate relationships with the Creator. A prominent talk-show host once stated that he sometimes felt as though his heart had a hole in it through which a cold wind blew. This statement describes the emptiness in the life of a person who does not have a meaningful relationship with God. In Genesis God inaugurated this relationship with human beings by walking with Adam and Eve in the cool of the evening. Humans possess an innate desire to glorify and worship the Creator. Wherever we find historical evidence of human existence, we find implements for worship. Anytime we define life and ignore this purpose, we will find life incomplete.

Solomon, the king of Israel, was one of the wealthiest and wisest men ever to live. In Ecclesiastes Solomon recorded his quest to find life's true meaning. The early chapters of that book describe his search for meaning through knowledge, work, pleasure, strong drink, and the accumulation of treasure. Where did Solomon's quest lead him? Ecclesiastes 2:11 is particularly insightful:

When I surveyed all that my hands had done
  and what I had toiled to achieve,
    everything was meaningless, a chasing after the wind;
      nothing was gained under the sun.

If the word *vanity* strikes a familiar chord, there is a good reason, as well as a good solution. Solomon found his accumulation of knowledge, pleasure, and wealth to be sheer vanity because he could not escape two undeniable truths about life. The first is that all life ultimately ends in death (see Eccl. 2:18). Death is no respecter of persons, and even the wealthy and successful will die. Death is certain, and all the accumulations of this life will hold no meaning after death.

The second undeniable truth that troubled Solomon was the evil of persons. Read this sad refrain:

Again I looked and saw all the oppression that was
  taking place under the sun:

    I saw the tears of the oppressed—
      and they have no comforter;
    power was on the side of their oppressors—
      and they have no comforter.
    And I declared that the dead,
      who had already died,
    are happier than the living,
      who are still alive.
    But better than both
      is he who has not yet been,
    who has not seen the evil
      that is done under the sun" (Eccl. 4:1-3).

If Solomon, among the wisest and wealthiest men who ever

lived, spent his entire life in the quest for meaning, then his conclusions have value for us. His foundational conclusion is found in Ecclesiastes 12:1:

> Remember your Creator
> in the days of your youth,
> before the days of trouble come
> and the years approach when you will say,
> "I find no pleasure in them."

After all his searching, Solomon discovered that he was created to have fellowship with his Creator and that life had no ultimate purpose or meaning apart from this relationship.

▼ THINK ABOUT IT

Circle the word or the phrase in the previous sentence that is the key to understanding your purpose in life.

Human beings were created for relationships with one another. Humankind was created male and female. In Genesis 2 we discover that God created them to complement and fulfill each other. Thus, the institution of marriage is not a social convenience but a divine plan. Beyond the relationship of husband and wife are family members and friends.

As Solomon sought to discover the meaning of life, he emphasized the significance of developing meaningful relationships:

> Two are better than one,
> because they have a good return for their work:
> If one falls down,
> his friend can help him up.
> But pity the man who falls

and has no one to help him up!
   Also, if two lie down together, they will keep warm.
     But how can one keep warm alone?
   Though one may be overpowered,
     two can defend themselves.
   A cord of three strands is not quickly broken
     (Eccl. 4:9-12).

By creation persons are relational beings; therefore, our purpose includes meaningful relationships.

▼HINK ABOUT IT

List the relationships that provide meaning for your life.

_____

_____

_____

_____

_____

Human beings were assigned the stewardship of the created order. Humankind's task is to use responsibly and care for the created earth. We are told that the earth as created was "very good" (Gen. 1:31). God placed all earth's resources at humans' disposal for their enjoyment and use. Thus, man and woman are called to work in fellowship with the Creator to rule over the entire created order. This has profound implications for humankind's care of the environment, as well as for scientific learning and exploration.

Solomon discovered that his labor could be meaningful and joyful when understood in the context of God's purpose: "A man can do nothing better than to eat and drink and find satisfaction in his work. This too, I see, is from the hand of God, for without him, who can eat or find enjoyment?" (Eccl. 2:24-25). When we understand that God, motivated by His love for us, created a good world, we respond with responsible and not abusive enjoyment. Further, when we see our work as commissioned by the Creator, life and work take on a new sense of dignity and purpose (see Eccl. 3:12-14a).

THINK ABOUT IT

Other than relationships with God and with others, what other task gives meaning to life?

_____

_____

_____

Our life matters! We are here by divine intention! Our threefold purpose centers in our relationship to the Creator. This, in turn, leads to meaningful relationships with others and to responsible stewardship of the created order. Notice that the biblical worldview includes the very best of what the world has to offer, but it is balanced. When we have a relationship with God, personal pleasure and happiness have real meaning. We can enjoy our work and the results of our work. The full realization of our human potential is made possible only when we discover our created purpose. Finally, our ability to live in relationship with others depends on our proper relationship with the Creator. He enables us to overcome the self-centeredness that causes us to neglect others' needs to satisfy our own needs.

The answer to the question, Why am I here? should have profound implications for the way we live; it should determine the values by which we live.

▼HINK ABOUT IT

Rewrite in your own words the three aspects of God's purpose for life.

1. _____

2. _____

3. _____

Do these statements reflect your purpose in life? If not, how does yours differ?

_____

_____

_____

_____

HOW SHALL I LIVE?

One Sunday morning I began my message while holding a softball. I asked the congregation, "What color is the ball?" They immediately answered, "White." Then I turned to the choir and asked if they agreed with the congregation. They immediately began shaking their heads, telling me that the ball was black. Both groups were correct; I had painted half of the ball black before bringing it to the pulpit.

Having illustrated that the ball's color was related to their perspective, I tossed the ball into the air and stated, "It actually looks gray when it spins quickly."

Many people view values in a similar manner, arguing that moral issues are relative. Right and wrong depend, they assert, on one's perspective. Who can say that homosexuality, adultery, lying, or cheating is wrong? Who has the authority to determine right and wrong?

Are moral values relative? Apparently, many Bible-believing Christians think so. People often ask me, "Pastor, I know it's not right for me to do this, but who am I to say that it's wrong for someone else?" Do absolutes exist? How do we determine values and thus decide how we should live?

When it comes to values, we have only two options. Values are either human-centered or God-centered.

HOW VALUES ARE FORMED

Option 1	Option 2
Human-Centered	God-Centered
Subjective	Objective
Relative	Absolute
Changing	Unchanging

Recall an earlier question: Where did we come from? If we are the result of a chance evolutionary process and the highest form of life, we should determine our own values. Then it truly is our decision how we should live, based on our particular life philosophy. This would mean that all values are relative, subjective, and changing. If, however, God created us, then only the Creator can establish the values by which we must live to fulfill His purpose.

How Does the World Determine Values?

If we deny absolute moral values, which God established as part of His revelation of Himself, then we are left to determine our own values. How do we go about this process? We might suggest the process of trial and error. If we use one form of behavior and it has undesirable consequences, then we avoid that behavior in the future. This certainly is a workable solution in some situations, such as touching a hot object, which produces pain and teaches us not to do this in the future. However, if we adopted such a method for determining how we should live, we would face devastating consequences in the process of finding livable values.

Some suggest that values should be based on what provides the greatest good in the long run. This is the basic premise of situation ethics. This enables a mother who determines that she cannot adequately care for the child she is carrying to decide that an abortion is the best choice in the long run. This system is always subjective, unconcerned with the welfare of other persons. In the previous example the abortion was based on what the mother determined was best for her. She may have argued that it was best for the baby also, but she has no power to decide that not living is best for another person.

We can determine values based on what works. If it works, do it. Again, we are left to our own ingenuity to determine what works best, and we usually seek what works best for us. Thus, it may not consider the interests of others.

We might decide that we should set moral values by societal vote. Thus, if 51 percent of society votes that we should conduct ourselves in a certain way, then that becomes the standard by which we live. This suggestion works well if we assume that people are just, kind, and loving in all their judgments. For example, if 51 percent of the populace determines that abortion on demand is acceptable, does that make it morally right? Before you answer that, think of the implications. If that judgment is correct, then Hitler's actions were justified. In the beginning of his reign a majority of the people supported Hitler. Yet sentiment changed, and he lost his support. Are we to conclude that his actions were morally acceptable in the beginning but not so at the end? Notice the relativity and changing nature of moral values if they are based in humans, individually or collectively.

▼HINK ABOUT IT

Following are the bases for determining values in our culture.
Choose the one you observe being used most often.

❑ Trial and error   ❑ Societal vote
❑ Apparent long-term benefits   ❑ Biblical truth
❑ What works

The ultimate flaw in human-centered values is that humans
themselves are flawed and cannot develop a system to preserve
human dignity and welfare. Humanists, pantheists, and even deists
deny absolutes; yet ironically, they accept that assertion as their
one absolute. Thus, they do not tolerate anyone who claims moral
absolutes.

▼HINK ABOUT IT

Check the main reason human-centered values are always flawed.
Read Romans 3:23 to find the answer.

❑ 1. Humans have limited intelligence.
❑ 2. Humans are too shortsighted.
❑ 3. Humans are inherently sinful.
❑ 4. Humans lack the capacity to love.

Did you choose number 3? Human-centered values are flawed
because humans are sinful.

Now take a careful look at the long-term ramifications of
human-centered values.

Human-centered values lead to moral chaos. If we have no
authority to establish absolutes, then all persons have equal rights
to their choices. There would be no difference between getting
drunk and being the leader of a nation! We have no basis for

evaluating the actions of a Hitler, a Manson, or a Dahmer. All three consistently lived by their own values. If humans establish the laws, if we transcend good and evil, if the laws are evolving, then we have no consistent basis for moral judgments. We cannot say that a drug lord is wrong or evil. In terms of his value system he is providing a service and making a living. Without an established moral basis how can we evaluate homosexuality, sexual promiscuity, or incest?

Human-centered values lead to societal disintegration. On this point the historical record is clear. Once the basis for moral absolutes is destroyed, the fabric of society begins to unravel. We begin to defend abortion, for instance, on the basis of women's rights. The short-term effect is justified because the unwanted child may grow up unloved or impoverished. We practice mercy killing because it relieves unnecessary suffering.

Human-centered values lead to the loss of individual rights. If people determine their own values, no guarantee exists for preserving individual rights. Ultimately, the strongest one wins. The woman's rights take priority over those of the unborn child because she is the stronger party in the negotiations. This system satisfies our human nature until we are the weaker party in the negotiations. Then we cry out for protection of our rights.

Do you remember the story of Robin Hood? When Robin Hood and Little John first met, they had an altercation because both wanted to cross a one-way log at the same time. Neither was willing to give in, and both asserted their rights to cross the log. Without rules to govern who should cross first, the outcome was settled by a fight and the survival of the fittest.

If values are always evolving and are always decided by humans, then ultimately, no one can be assured of individual rights, particularly when they impinge on the rights of another. The issue of moral values is basic to the organization of society. It is not surprising that Satan's most frequent tactic is to tempt persons to question and rebel against God's law.

Circle in the foregoing text the three long-term ramifications of human-centered values. Choose one and write examples that you have observed in your community.

_____

_____

_____

_____

_____

What Is the Biblical Alternative?
The writer of Proverbs gave wise counsel:

> Trust in the Lord with all your heart
> and lean not on your own understanding (Prov. 3:5).

As creations designed by the Creator, we have a specific purpose: to live in relationship with Him and other persons and to manage and enjoy the created world. If we are to accomplish our given purpose, we must do so by living in harmony with the Creator's natural and moral laws. We must live in a manner that pleases Him. We have no meaningful purpose outside His purpose.

This insight alone makes evangelism the evangelical believer's number one priority. It is critical that we lead people to Christ so that they not only can go to heaven but also can live with purpose in this life. The difference between the strategy of a Peace Corps volunteer and that of a missionary is evident. The Peace Corps worker feeds the hungry, teaches them how to grow crops, and concludes that the task is complete. The missionary feeds them, teaches them how to grow crops, and attempts to lead them to meaningful relationships with their Creator. Evangelism becomes a mandate because the only way people are ultimately fulfilled is to live in harmony with their Creator, the God of the Bible.

If our priority task is to live according to God's design, where do we find such information? Recall our second axiom: "God reveals Himself." We should look to God's revelation of Himself, the Bible, for instruction on how to live. God's law expresses both the nature of God and His love for His creation. Since God created the world and us, a perfect relationship exists between what is and what ought to be. Moral obligation flows from God's will for us. Christ's coming in no way negates the validity of God's moral law. Jesus stated that He came to fulfill the law, not to destroy it. His coming and the accompanying indwelling of the Spirit enable individuals to obey the law.

Ethics based solely on biblical revelation provides a system perfectly balanced to meet all our needs, like a balanced and nutritious meal. For this reason, we cannot choose the terms of our obedience. God's law is unique for six reasons:

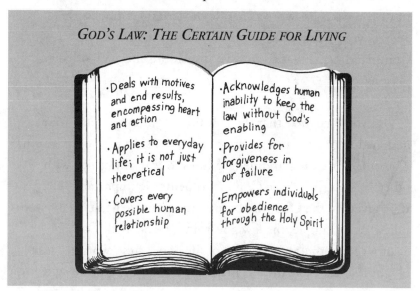

GOD'S LAW: THE CERTAIN GUIDE FOR LIVING

- Deals with motives and end results, encompassing heart and action

- Applies to everyday life; it is not just theoretical

- Covers every possible human relationship

- Acknowledges human inability to keep the law without God's enabling

- Provides for forgiveness in our failure

- Empowers individuals for obedience through the Holy Spirit

The Ten Commandments, found in Exodus 20:3-17, are the heart of biblical ethics, as well as the foundation of most civil law in our country. Each of the Ten Commandments is expressed in the second-person singular, calling every individual in the community to bear responsibility for obedience. Being under grace does not mean that the Ten Commandments are not applicable to us. Grace gives us freedom, joy, and power for obedience. Let's look at these codes for purposeful human relationships.

1. You shall have no other gods before me.
2. You shall not make for yourself an idol.
3. You shall not misuse the name of the Lord your God.
4. Remember the Sabbath day by keeping it holy.
5. Honor your father and your mother.
6. You shall not murder.
7. You shall not commit adultery.
8. You shall not steal.
9. You shall not give false testimony.
10. You shall not covet.

▼THINK ABOUT IT

In the previous list write *G* beside the Commandments that address your relationship with God. Write *R* beside the Commandments that address your relationships with other persons.

Did you recognize that the first four Commandments were designed to protect and govern our relationship with our Creator? The other six Commandments address our relationships with other persons. All of the Commandments are important. They were given by the One who created us to enable us to live life to its fullest. For example, the law governing the Sabbath Day acknowledges the basic rhythm of life: work, rest, worship. Jesus taught that the Sabbath was made for persons. A gracious gift from the Creator, it recognizes our need to be spiritually and physically renewed and reminds us that all time belongs to God. The Commandment that prohibits stealing protects our right to own property and thus prohibits the taking of another person's property. Stealing is a sin not only against others but also against God. It betrays our trust in Him to provide for our needs.

Do you realize what is at stake here? The very fabric of our society. God's law must be allowed to permeate our thinking about every institution and relationship in life. Work, family, church, body, political involvement, art, science—all arenas of our lives must be placed under God's law. Our loving Father provided it so we could enjoy life to its fullest.

Dualism: The belief that evil and good are coexistent and equal forces.

Finitism: The belief that God is limited and cannot affect some circumstances.

Karma: A law of cause and effect claiming that every decision an individual makes in the present is caused by all prior decisions and will affect every future decision.

5

WHY DOES EVIL EXIST?

The ringing of the telephone disrupted his thoughts as he pored over his Sunday School lesson. The interruption was a welcome reprieve. He was preparing to teach the story about the woman of Samaria and was struggling to understand the phrase *living water.* But once the caller identified himself and proceeded with his message, time froze! "There has been a flood at the Bible college, and your parents are dead."

Flood Claims Lives of Missionaries

Tragedy struck at a local Bible college, the result of flooding from severe thunderstorms. Two fatalities were reported earlier today.

There must be some mistake! God could not allow a natural catastrophe to happen to such good people. They are missionaries, humble and godly persons. They've given their lives in selfless service, and now they are dead. It doesn't seem fair.

Yet it was true; they were gone.

They were happy beyond measure—a picture-perfect couple. From the beginning they had seemed ideally suited for each other and had fallen deeply in love. During premarital counseling they had made a commitment to Christ and had joined our church. Their growth had been rapid and obvious. They had joined a couples' class and had soon become care-group leaders. She was a popular teacher at a local high school, and he was a well-respected businessman.

None of us were prepared for the jolting

Local Teacher Murdered

A local teacher was raped and killed in her home late last night. Suspects include a friend of the family who had stopped by for assistance.

message that shocked the entire community. She was dead! While the husband was away on a business trip, a man they had befriended in the past stopped by for assistance. Sensing her vulnerability, he forced his way into the house, then raped and killed the lovely, innocent teacher.

Why? Who is to blame? Where was God? Can He do anything about such evil? If God is an all-powerful and an all-loving God, then in some way He must be implicated in such events. Right?

Why are babies born with physical defects? Why do children die? Why does war rage? Why do people starve? How do we explain the pain and suffering in the world around us?

Not all events are as dramatic as these, but we all know of similar stories that cause us to question the goodness or the power of God in the face of evil. Evil does exist. We read about it daily in the newspaper and hear about it on the evening news: "Teenager Slays Two Friends," "High-speed Chase Ends in Crash," "Hundreds Die as Tornado Rips Coastline." Headlines such as these are so commonplace that they no longer shock us.

Moral evils, such as rape, murder, drug abuse, and mass slayings, seem to be growing at astounding rates. *Natural evils*, such as killer tornadoes and earthquakes, are evidences of the reality of evil.

THINK ABOUT IT

Describe a recent tragedy in your community that illustrates the reality of evil.

_____

_____

Have you experienced a personal tragedy or loss that caused you to question your own faith seriously? Write a brief account of this experience.

_____

_____

_____

How did you reconcile your personal faith with those circumstances?

_____

_____

_____

HOW DO WE EXPLAIN EVIL?

How do we explain the presence of evil? Frequently, this question is hurled at Christians in an accusatory manner by someone who asks how a completely good and all-powerful God could permit evil. Even some persons who do not believe in God accuse Him of causing evil events. They conclude that they cannot believe in a God who would permit such tragedy and needless suffering. Such circular reasoning is sometimes hard to follow, but it challenges us nonetheless to be ready to answer the skeptic.

We must ask whether the Christian worldview can offer a practical, cogent, and meaningful answer to the problem of evil. Does the Christian faith make sense of our world? Remember, however, that any worldview must confront and answer this same question. Can the humanist or the pantheist explain and resolve the problem of evil? Does the New Age proponent possess answers to this question?

We have three options in seeking to explain the coexistence of God and evil.

THREE ANSWERS TO THE QUESTION OF EVIL

God exists, and evil does not exist	God exists, and evil exists	Evil exists, and God does not exist
Hinduism Christian Science Pantheism	Theism	Atheism

We could argue that God exists and that evil does not. This is the position of Hinduism and Christian Science. On the other end of the spectrum is the argument that evil exists and that God does not. This is the classic argument of atheism. Between these two extremes is the possibility that both God and evil exist. Let's take a closer look at each of the three options for the coexistence of God and evil.[1]

God Exists, and Evil Does Not Exist

This view claims that evil is an illusion and does not actually exist. Some Eastern religions, including forms of Hinduism, argue that evil is an illusion. This assertion is based on the belief that everything is one (monism) and good. Therefore, all seeming departures from good are illusions. The pantheist believes that God is all and all is God. Thus, since God is good, all is good. This philosophical system has begun to influence Western thought through New Age thinking. New Age thinking is also based on the monistic belief that God is all and we are part of God.

A more familiar example is the teaching of Christian Science. Its founder, Mary Baker Eddy, wrote: "Evil is but an illusion, and it has no real basis."[2] Eddy argued that evil is not real, only an error of the mortal mind. Thus, she maintained that sin, sickness, and death are mortal illusions and actually do not exist.

How are we to evaluate the argument that evil does not exist? To accept this proposition, we must deny the evidence of our senses and our personal experiences. We might ask, Why is the illusion of evil so real and so universal? We see and experience suffering and evil. If we deny the reality of these evil occurrences, can we trust our senses in any area of life and thinking? Do we disregard all the scientific and historical evidence that points to the real existence of evil, pain, and suffering? Do we argue that the Civil War and the Holocaust were illusions? How do we convince the families of those killed in these illusions that the evil events never happened? Would such a suggestion be comforting? If evil and its accompanying suffering are illusions, then millions of dollars expended on medical research to discover ways to alleviate suffering are wasted.

Few persons can consistently maintain the belief that evil is an illusion. Would you refuse to take your daughter to a hospital if she had been in a tragic accident? Would you pick up her broken body and assert that the apparent injuries are mere illusions, resulting from false thinking?

An attempt to deny the existence of evil is only wishful thinking, not a valid solution to the problem of evil.

THINK ABOUT IT

Do you think the idea that evil does not exist has any merit? Why or why not?

_____

_____

_____

_____

_____

Evil Exists, and God Does Not Exist

The argument that evil exists and God does not exist is at the opposite end of the spectrum. This is the atheist's argument. The atheist does not have a problem with evil. For the atheist, evil, death, and suffering are guaranteed. If the world operates strictly according to the process of evolution, which the atheist must accept, then the survival of the fittest is inherent in the system. It is this presence of evil, the atheist argues, that proves that God does not exist. If God is all-good and all-powerful, then He has a moral obligation to remove evil. Since evil exists, the atheist reasons, God does not exist.

However, this conclusion is flawed. It assumes that evil would have been destroyed by now if God were all-good and all-powerful. Is it possible that evil is in the process of being defeated? Could God have a reason for permitting evil to operate until it is ultimately destroyed? Since God has not completely destroyed evil, must we assume that He never will?

Note that atheism offers no solution for the problem of evil. It accepts evil as an inevitable part of the evolutionary process. Actually, for an atheist or a humanist to fight against evil is a contradiction since evil is inherent in the system. Why work to save a nearly extinct species since such extinction is an inevitable part of the evolutionary system? In truth, it is more difficult for the atheist to account for the presence of good than for the Christian to account for evil.

Atheism and its philosophical counterpart, atheistic humanism, are negative positions that only serve to argue that God does not exist. True atheism is fatalistic and hopeless. It has no real solution for evil and sin. Any struggle against evil is a futile attempt to swim against the inevitable current of the evolutionary process.

Living with such a hopeless worldview is difficult. This futile view of life and evil is clearly reflected in much of today's music and art. A quick trip through a local gallery proves that many people see the world as confused, violent, and hopeless. Our oldest daughter is a talented artist, and we have attended local competitions with her. Often we are dismayed to see the dissonant and destructive nature of many artistic creations. If you hear or read contemporary music, you will be troubled by the messages of evil and futility expressed in the lyrics. The growing problem of teen suicide may relate to the hopelessness of the atheistic worldview.

▼THINK ABOUT IT

Do you think the idea that evil exists and God does not exist has any merit? Why or why not?

_____

_____

_____

_____

_____

God Exists, and Evil Exists

If we cannot deny the existence of God and evil, how do we resolve the tension of the existence of an all-powerful and all-good God and the presence of evil? Three attempts have been made to resolve this apparent problem.

God and evil are opposite and equal. This position, called dualism, is based on the argument that nothing can be the source of its opposite. The dualist accepts evil as a real entity in itself but the opposite of God, who is good. Thus, the dualist concludes that both good and evil must have existed together from all eternity.

This idea is seen in the symbol of the yin and yang, a Chinese concept of the two eternal opposites of good and evil.

This view may help picture the existence of evil, but it does not help resolve the problem of evil. If both God and evil are coeternal opposites, what hope do we have that God can overcome evil?

Dualism is not only hopeless but also flawed in its thinking and untenable. First, a seemingly evil circumstance can result from something that is not inherently evil. While driving a car, we may innocently and accidentally strike a pedestrian. There is nothing inherently evil in driving a car, but a bad thing happens as a result. Also, the fact that evil and good are opposites does not mean that they have always existed as eternal opposites. Finally, this suggestion of coeternal and equal opposites is not logical. If one day good will overcome evil, then they were never coeternal and equal opposites.

Dualism is built on a false assumption. It assumes that evil is a thing and has an existence of its own. Yet no evidence exists that evil has an existence of its own. Evil can be better understood as a corruption of something good that already exists or a privation of that good. Blindness, for example, is the lack of sight where there should be sight. Rust, rot, and decay are simply the corruption of good things. When evil is not present in a thing, that thing is better. When you take away all good from something, nothing is left at all. "Evil does not exist by itself, because it does not exist apart from good."[3]

▼THINK ABOUT IT

Check each statement that reveals a flaw of dualism.

❑ 1. Evil can result from something that is not inherently evil.
❑ 2. Evil is not eternal.
❑ 3. Evil does not have a life of its own.
❑ 4. Evil is real.

You should have checked 1, 2, and 3.

Evil is greater than God. Some have resolved the problem of the coexistence of God and evil by arguing that God exists but that He is finite, lacking the power to control or stop evil. This idea is called finitism because it views God as a finite being who struggles with the problem of evil as we do. If evil is to be destroyed, we must join God in the fight. This concept has provided some persons the motivation to work against social evil, since God depends on our actions for final victory. Some proponents claim that they find it easier to relate to a limited God.

This position has serious problems. If God is limited, then He is finite. Therefore, He is not God, since every finite being must be caused, and God, by definition, is the uncaused Cause. If God had sufficient power to create the world, why would He create a world in which He knew that He could not control evil? Some have attempted to absolve God by asserting that He simply did not foresee the potential for evil. In that case we must assume that God is not all-knowing and is finite, not infinite. How could a finite God assure us that good will finally triumph? If God Himself cannot check the forces of evil, then what hope do mortals have of doing so?[4]

The view of a finite God who is powerless to resolve evil has been popularized by Rabbi Kushner in his book *When Bad Things Happen to Good People.* Rabbi Kushner had accepted the traditional Jewish view of God as all-good and all-powerful until the tragic death of his son caused him to question his traditional beliefs. Kushner based his conclusions on a study of the Book of Job, stating that a good person like Job did not deserve to experience such terrible misfortunes. Why, then, did he still suffer? Kushner stated, "God wants the righteous to live peaceful, happy lives, but sometimes even He can't bring that about."[5] In other words, God is limited in what He can accomplish. God is not perfect, as the imperfect world clearly demonstrates.

Kushner claims to find a sense of relief in the discovery that

God is limited and therefore not the cause of our misfortunes: "I can worship a God who hates suffering but cannot eliminate it, more easily than I can worship a God who chooses to make children suffer and die, for whatever exalted reason."[6]

Why, then, does evil occur? Kushner offers several suggestions. Some evil events are caused by bad luck, others by bad people. The inflexible laws of nature create some evil events, while the randomness in the universe can be blamed for others.

Finitism does not offer a satisfactory answer to the question of evil, and it makes God in our own image. If God cannot overcome evil, then we live in a hopeless situation.

▼HINK ABOUT IT

Check each statement that reveals a flaw of finitism.

❑ 1. God is limited and therefore finite.
❑ 2. God is all-knowing, including knowledge about evil.
❑ 3. God did not foresee the problem of evil.
❑ 4. God cannot overcome some evil.

You should have checked 1, 3, and 4.

God is greater than evil and will destroy it. This is a summary of biblical theism. Biblical theism argues that an all-powerful and all-good God has provided both an immediate and a long-term solution to the problem of evil. We can follow a step-by-step process to understand the theistic answer to the question of the existence of evil in a good creation and how the problem of evil will finally be resolved.

Step 1: God's creation is good. God created the world and all that is in it from nothing. His creation was good (see Gen. 1:31). God is not the author of evil.

Step 2: Human beings were created in the image of God and were given free will (see Gen. 1:27; 2:16-17). All created things by definition have the possibility of corruption and nonexistence since they are created and therefore finite. Every created thing can be destroyed!

Step 3: Free choice necessitates the possibility of choosing evil. Free choice is in itself a good gift of God, but along with it comes the possibility of choosing evil. Humans' free choice was the point at which evil entered God's good creation. Notice that evil was the corruption of a good thing (free choice). The presence of choice does not necessitate evil, but it allows for the possibility of disobedience and the accompanying evil. If there had not been disobedience, there would not be a problem with evil. Paul wrote in Romans 5:12, "Just as sin entered the world through one man, and death through sin, and in this way death came to all men, because all sinned."

A parent permits a child to make choices. That child may make wrong choices, bringing unnecessary evil and suffering on himself and others. The child was not coerced into choosing wrongly. We would not blame the parent for the child's wrong choice simply because the parent had provided the opportunity for choice.

Some persons might ask why God did not create the world so that we could not choose evil. Could we really say that people have free choice if they are not able to choose evil? If we visited an ice-cream parlor that advertised 32 choices only to find that all the choices were vanilla, we would rightly complain that we had no choice.

The opportunity to choose is essential to a moral universe. If free will did not exist, we would be little more than robots or preprogrammed androids. As such, we would be incapable of either good or evil. Obedience that is programmed or coerced is not really the loving response that God desires.

THINK ABOUT IT

Mark the following statements *T* for true or *F* for false.

__ 1. God is the author of evil.

__ 2. Being created means that all humans are finite.

__ 3. Free choice is a good gift from God.

__ 4. To eliminate evil would necessitate God's removing our free will.

__ 5. Without free will, true love and obedience would not be possible.

Answers: 1. F, 2. T, 3. T, 4. T, 5. T.

Step 4: The human choice to sin has affected the entire created order. Paul stated in Romans 8:20-21: "The creation was subjected to frustration, not by its own choice, but by the will of the one who subjected it, in hope that the creation itself will be liberated from its bondage to decay and brought into the glorious freedom of the children of God." Thus, we see, for example, the effect of human sin in the pollution and desecration of the environment, which cause human suffering.

Step 5: Evil cannot be fully understood without recognizing the reality of an evil adversary (see Gen. 3:1-15). The Bible does not give a complete answer to the question of Satan's origin. Apparently, Satan was created a beautiful angelic being. Along with other angelic beings, Satan chose to rebel against God (see 2 Pet. 2:4; Jude 6). The New Testament pictures Satan as a rebel against God. He and his angels became the enemies of God and humanity, apparently of their free will. Satan is the deceiver and accuser of humankind (see Rev. 12:9-10). He tempts us to yield to our fleshly desires and then accuses us of our failure, creating unhealthy guilt.

Step 6: God will totally and finally defeat evil. The apostle Paul looked with great hope to a final defeat of all evil. He clearly expressed this hope in Romans 8:18: "I consider that our present sufferings are not worth comparing with the glory that will be revealed in us."

▼HINK ABOUT IT

Write a sentence that expresses what you believe Paul meant by his words in Romans 8:18.

_____

_____

_____

I am certain that you noticed that Paul contrasted present sufferings with ultimate glory, concluding that there is really no comparison.

Now read Romans 8:20-21: "The creation was subjected to frustration, not by its own choice, but by the will of the one who subjected it, in hope that the creation itself will be liberated from its bondage to decay and brought into the glorious freedom of the children of God."

Write a sentence expressing what you believe these verses mean.

_____

_____

_____

_____

You probably noted that these verses teach that all creation, including the forces of nature, will be liberated from the curse of evil.

The Book of Revelation often speaks of this final triumph over evil and its personal results. Look, for example, at Revelation 21:3-4: "I heard a loud voice from the throne saying, 'Now the dwelling of God is with men, and he will live with them. They will be his people, and God himself will be with them and be their God. He will wipe every tear from their eyes. There will be no more death or mourning or crying or pain, for the old order of things has passed away.' "

List things in these verses that will no longer be a problem for God's people when they are with Him forever.

_____

_____

_____

_____

_____

You probably listed items like tears, death, mourning, and pain, which will be defeated forever. These negative and hurtful things belong to the old order, which will pass away. These things will no longer trouble us when we are with the Lord. God will finally and forever triumph over all of them.

Step 7: God's gift of free will prevents the present removal of evil. You undoubtedly agree that freedom from evil and suffering in the future will be glorious, but what about suffering in the present? How can evil ever be reconciled with God's will? Why does God not simply destroy all evil now?

Usually when we ask these questions, we conveniently ignore our own evil. Do we want Him to remove our free will and program us for good? To remove sin without destroying us would require that freedom be eliminated. Since freedom is essential to a moral universe, such an action would result in an amoral universe. If God removed our freedom of choice, we would no longer be made in His image. Without free will we would no longer have the option to love God or others.

If God destroyed all evil, He would annihilate the entire human race, including ourselves, since "all have sinned" (Rom. 3:23). God is patient. He does not want anyone to be lost (see 2 Pet. 3:9). Therefore, He permits the existence of evil, in patience, so all might have the chance to fulfill their eternal destinies by living in relationship with the Creator. When we grieve over the reality of evil, we should think about how much it must grieve the heart of the Creator, who made it all very good. It must hurt to see His creation spoiled and desecrated.

Step 8: God dealt with the problem of evil by sending His Son to pay the penalty for sin. "All have sinned" (Rom. 3:23), and "the wages of sin is death" (Rom. 6:23). We all deserve to die. Yet God sent His own Son in human flesh. We call the coming of Jesus in human flesh the incarnation. Jesus was a man in every sense of the word but lived without sin. He died on a cross to pay the penalty for our sin: "God made him who had no sin to be sin for us, so that in him we might become the righteousness of God" (2 Cor. 5:21).

THINK ABOUT IT

To whom was Paul referring when he wrote of "him who had no sin"?

_____

_____

_____

Can it truthfully be said of anyone who has ever lived, other than Jesus, that he or she had no sin? Yes ____   No ____

What do you believe Paul meant when he wrote, "God made him who had no sin to be sin for us, so that in him we might become the righteousness of God"?

_____

_____

_____

_____

_____

_____

The truth of this passage has been illustrated in several different ways. Two college friends who had not seen each other in years met in a courtroom. One was the judge and the other the defendant. As the trial progressed, it became apparent that the accused was guilty as charged, but he still had hope because the judge was his friend. When the time came for the verdict to be announced, he was shocked because the judge declared him to be guilty and set a stiff fine. After sentencing him, the judge removed his robe, stepped down from his chair, and voluntarily paid his fine, thus satisfying the requirement of the law. The judge's sense of justice required that he pass sentence; his grace and mercy prompted him to pay the penalty. That is precisely what God did for us when He sent His Son to pay the penalty of our sin.

You may have memorized John 3:16 long ago, but take a fresh look at it now: "God so loved the world that He gave his one and only Son, that whoever believes in him shall not perish but have eternal life." It has been correctly said that any person can insert his or her name in place of the word *world*. The verse is just as true when you make that change.

▼HINK ABOUT IT

Try that right now. Write your name in the blanks:

"God so loved _____ that he gave his one and only Son that [if] _____ believes in him, _____ shall not perish but have eternal life."

Romans 8:16-17 has a powerful promise for those who have accepted God's great love and have experienced the forgiveness of sin in Jesus Christ: "The Spirit himself testifies with our spirit that we are God's children. Now if we are children, then we are heirs— heirs of God and co-heirs with Christ, if indeed we share in his sufferings in order that we may also share in his glory." We are heirs of God and coheirs with Christ.

▼HINK ABOUT IT

The heirs of a wealthy person will someday inherit that person's wealth. If we, along with Jesus, are heirs of God, this means that (check the best answer)—

❑ God owns everything, but we are destined to poverty and defeat for eternity;

❑ all the riches of God will be ours someday because we are His heirs.

These verses teach that Christ shares our sufferings. In the future He will share His glory with us. We can be assured that all evil and its accompanying suffering will one day be vindicated.

Let me ask you a personal question. Do you know for certain that you have eternal life? I'm not asking if you are a religious person or attend church. Have you admitted your sinfulness and accepted Christ as the payment for your sin by inviting Him to come into your heart and to be your Lord and Savior? If not, why not do so right now?

Prayer is simply talking to God. Tell Him now that you want to receive Jesus as the payment for your sin. Read this prayer and decide whether it says what you desire to say to God.

> Dear God, I know that Jesus is Your Son and that He died on the cross and was raised from the dead. I know that I have sinned and need forgiveness. I am willing to turn from my sins and to receive Jesus as my Savior and Lord. Thank You for saving me. In Jesus' name. Amen.

If you prayed that prayer and are willing to turn over your life to Jesus Christ, you can be confident that your sins have been forgiven and that you are a child of God. I encourage you to tell a Christian friend or the pastor of a Bible-teaching church that you decided to trust Christ. This person should help you become a part of a fellowship of other believers and should help you understand what it means to be a Christian.

Step 9: When evil brings suffering, God cares, promises His presence, and promises to bring good from evil. Although we will consider personal suffering later, for now we will examine a Bible promise that can sustain us through every circumstance of life: "We know that in all things God works for the good of those who love him, who have been called according to his purpose" (Rom. 8:28). This verse does not say that everything is good. It does not ignore the problem of evil and suffering. Instead, this verse promises that God will work through every circumstance to bring good to those who love Him.

WHAT ABOUT SUFFERING?

The question of suffering is a separate but related issue. It is often tied to the problem of evil with questions such as: Why do bad things happen to good people? What does God have against me? What wrong did I do to deserve this? Why does suffering come? Where is God when we suffer? These are valid, practical questions for which the Bible alone provides satisfactory answers.

Why Do We Suffer?

Many have asked this important question. It becomes very real when it results from painful experiences. Let's examine some of the answers to that question.

> ### REASONS FOR SUFFERING
> • The evil and bad decisions of others
> • The fallen state of creation
> • Bad choices
> • The work of the adversary
> • The operation of natural laws
> • The sake of righteousness
> • A mystery

Suffering results from the evil and bad decisions of others. A drunk driver crosses the lane and hits another car, causing injury and suffering. A father abuses his daughter, who suffers because of her father's sinful decision. The laziness of parents creates a financial situation that inflicts suffering on the entire family. These sinful actions of others may cause innocent people to suffer.

Yet again we must remember that if God eliminated free will, He would eliminate our opportunity to know and experience Him, which is our very reason for being.

Suffering results from the fallen state of creation. Reread Paul's words in Romans 8:21: "The creation itself will be liberated from its bondage to decay and brought into the glorious freedom of the children of God." When sin entered the world, it profoundly affected the entire created order. After the fall in the garden, Adam was told that the fruitful ground had been cursed so that it would bear thorns and thistles (see Gen. 3:18). The woman is told that she would have increased pains in childbirth (see Gen. 3:16). What is true of the human family is true of the entire created order. Because of sin's impact, genetic defects and natural catastrophes are possibilities and realities.

Suffering results from bad choices. Suffering is often inherent in the choices we make. For example, the smoker risks cancer; the user of alcohol may develop cirrhosis of the liver; and the overeater may find that the extra weight affects physical well-being. Someone who commits sexual sin risks serious disease, unwanted pregnancy, and deep psychological scarring. An angry God does not cause these results that produce suffering. The risks are inherent in the disobedient act. If you choose to disobey the traffic signals and step into the path of an oncoming truck, you will suffer the results. This is what Paul meant in Romans 1:27 when he declared that those committing indecent and disobedient sexual acts would receive the due penalty of the error in their own flesh. The sinful act itself would open them to the inherent consequences of the act. God's laws are designed to protect us from such unnecessary suffering. This is why obedience to God's law is so important to abundant living.

Suffering results from the work of the adversary. Remember that Satan's desire is to kill, steal, and destroy. The Gadarene demoniac described in Matthew 8 was suffering because of the acts of a demon. Job's suffering was directly related to the work of the adversary. We should also realize that satanic activity may relate to our sinful choices.

Suffering results from the operation of natural laws. The rain that brings the harvest can also bring devastating floods. This cause may also relate to the fallen state of the created order.

Suffering can be for the sake of righteousness. Jesus is the perfect example of a righteous person who suffered at the hands of evildoers. You may lose a job because you reported a colleague for stealing. That righteous act brought you undeserved suffering. When you suffer for righteousness, remember Jesus' words: " 'Blessed are those who are persecuted because of righteousness, for theirs is the kingdom of heaven' " (Matt. 5:10).

Suffering is sometimes a mystery. We desire to be perfect in our understanding, but we do not always clearly understand everything that happens in life.

▼THINK ABOUT IT

In the following list of reasons for suffering, write *Y* beside the suffering that humans can control. Write *N* beside that which we cannot control.

___ 1. The evil and bad decisions of others

___ 2. The fallen state of creation

___ 3. Bad choices

___ 4. The work of the adversary

___ 5. The operation of natural laws

___ 6. The sake of righteousness

___ 7. A mystery

Answers: 1. N, 2. N, 3. Y, 4. Y and N, 5. N, 6. N, 7. N.

Does God Care When We Suffer?

When we suffer, does God really care? Does He do anything to help us? According to a humanistic worldview, we must accept suffering as inevitable. A pantheist either denies suffering as wrong thinking or sees it as the result of actions in the previous life (the law of karma). Those who believe in the law of karma do little to alleviate pain and suffering since that would interfere with karmic justice.

Only the Bible provides helpful answers. Carefully read Romans 8:26-28: "The Spirit helps us in our weakness. We do not know what we ought to pray for, but the Spirit himself intercedes for us with groans that words cannot express. And he who searches our hearts knows the mind of the Spirit, because the Spirit intercedes for the saints in accordance with God's will. And we know that in all things God works for the good of those who love him, who have been called according to his purpose."

▼**T**HINK **A**BOUT **I**T
This passage indicates ways God participates in our suffering. Can you identify at least three ways?

1. _____

2. _____

3. _____

Compare your list to mine:

> ### *GOD PARTICIPATES IN OUR SUFFERING*
> • Helps us in our weaknesses
> • Gives us the Spirit to intercede for us
> • Works in everything for our good
> • Promises that nothing can separate us from Him

God helps us in our weaknesses (see Rom. 8:26). He is not aloof from our suffering. He grieves with us as a parent would grieve over a wounded child. Paul made the same point in a different way in 1 Corinthians 10:13: "God is faithful; he will not let you be tempted beyond what you can bear. But when you are tempted, he will also provide a way out so that you can stand up under it." God gives us supernatural strength to endure the suffering. We often hear believers say, "If not for God's strength, I couldn't have endured."

God gives us the Spirit to intercede for us (see Rom. 8:26-27). Sometimes in our suffering we are at a loss for words and truly do not know how to pray. God has not left us alone but has sent the Holy Spirit to intercede for us. Last year the shocking news came that my dad had a malignant brain tumor that required immediate surgery. I left for home late that evening. I was shocked and grieved, not knowing enough to pray intelligently. Yet as I expressed my pain to the Father, a calm assurance came over me, and I knew that the Holy Spirit was interceding for me.

God works in everything for our good (see Rom. 8:28). The verse does not say that God causes all things, for God cannot cause evil. It says that God works redemptively in all things. Remember that God's concept of what is good for us may differ from ours. God's ultimate desire is to make us like His Son. This is a point at which we really test the strength of our worldview. Do you believe that the highest aim in life is to please your Creator and to live in perfect relationship with Him? Or do you think that the goal of life is to be happy, comfortable, and free of pain? Sometimes our goal of comfort and God's desire for our glorification collide. How, you might ask, does God work for my good even in suffering, whatever the cause? Let me suggest a few ways.

He grows us in the image of His Son. All of Scripture affirms the truth that if we are to be like Christ in His glory, we must join Him in His suffering. Paul prayed that he might know the fellowship of His sufferings so that he might attain to the resurrection from the dead (see Phil. 3:10-11). In Romans 5:3-5

Paul explained how suffering and tribulation could lead to growth: "We also rejoice in our sufferings, because we know that suffering produces perseverance; perseverance, character; and character, hope. And hope does not disappoint us, because God has poured out his love into our hearts by the Holy Spirit, whom he has given us." In our antiseptic and sedated culture we want growth without pain. Much popular preaching would have us believe that being joined with Christ guarantees health and prosperity rather than suffering.

Suffering is often a point of revelation. Suffering sometimes enables us to understand more of God's purpose for our lives. Hosea, an Old Testament prophet, gained new insight through the suffering caused by an unfaithful wife. The apostle Paul also testified to this reality in 2 Corinthians 12:8-9, praying that God would remove the thorn from his flesh. The thorn was not removed, but Paul came to a deeper understanding of the sufficiency of God's grace. Often suffering brings out the best in people. The story of Joni Eareckson Tada has become well known. A quadriplegic, she is an accomplished artist, author, and speaker. If we allow God to work with us for good, suffering can be a point of revelation.

Suffering often keeps us from greater evil. As you read the Old Testament, you will frequently see occasions when suffering kept Israel from greater evil. For example, Joseph suffered separation from his family so that Israel would not have to suffer the ravages of the famine. I've seen immediate suffering save some of our singles from disastrous marriages. I have counseled persons who were crushed when a meaningful relationship had been broken by the other party. They experienced real pain. But as time progressed and they saw the unfolding of the other person's character, the injured party praised God that the small pain prevented greater injury.

Suffering is part of the probationary period of life. As believers, we already have citizenship in heaven, where we will have perfect, unhindered fellowship with the Father. Our present experience has meaning precisely because we are being transformed into Christ's image; our faith is being tested and purified: "In this you greatly rejoice, though now for a little while you may have had to suffer grief in all kinds of trials. These have come so that your faith—of greater worth than gold, which perishes even though refined by fire—may be proved genuine and may result in praise, glory and honor when Jesus Christ is revealed" (1 Pet. 1:6-7). If we could avoid all suffering, we would relinquish opportunities to develop more mature faith.

Suffering often provides a platform for witnessing. Heroic faith through suffering gives a powerful testimony to God's power to sustain His children. Corrie Ten Boom, a seemingly obscure woman, has touched the lives of millions by sharing the testimony of God's provision during her imprisonment in Hitler's reign. Joni Eareckson Tada's physical disability has provided a worldwide platform for declaring God's grace. Joseph suffered because of his brothers' evil decision and yet was given an opportunity to witness to God's sovereignty in a pagan nation. Take a moment and think of persons in your church who have touched your life because of heroic witnessing through suffering.

God suffers with us. He has already paid the greatest price to relieve suffering permanently. He sent His Son, who voluntarily suffered the penalty of our sin. If He loved us this much, we can know that He participates in our suffering. We err when in suffering we aim anger at our gracious Father, who gave His Son for us, who gave us His Spirit to intercede on our behalf, and who justifies us.

David B. Biebel in *If God Is So Good, Why Do I Hurt So Bad?* tells the story of his reaction to the news that his son Christopher was probably suffering from the same genetic disease that had killed his first son, Jonathan. He describes the pain that engulfed him and records his agonized cry: "If that's the way it's going to be, then God can go to hell." While driving to his parents' home to relay the devastating news, he suddenly realized that God had already gone to hell, in the person of Jesus, to redeem this sinful world.[7]

Several years ago a popular and vivacious schoolteacher from our congregation was brutally murdered. Her funeral was packed with her students, many of whom were angry at God. I told them that it was OK for them to be angry but that their anger was misdirected. Jesus came to give life! It is Satan who came to steal, kill, and destroy. We should be angry at sin.

God promises that nothing can separate us from Him (see Rom. 8:35-39). Paul looked at the intense suffering caused by persecution, famine, and peril and concluded that in all these things we are more than conquerors because we know that none of these can separate us from God's love. One of my favorite stories from the Olympics revolves around the gold-medal-winning diver Greg Louganis. After previously colliding with the board on a platform dive, he was asked in an interview to identify his last thought before he launched his medal-winning dive. His reply was fascinating: "My last thought was that no matter how I hit this dive, my mom will still love me."

Even though God, in His mercy, does not desire to destroy humankind, evil still remains. Suffering is real, and it causes pain. Ask yourself, *What would be the worst thing that could happen to me in my present suffering?* You could lose your job, your family, your health, or even your life. But if you have a personal relationship with God through His Son, you can never lose that relationship. One day there will be no more suffering and pain. Until then you can rest assured that nothing, absolutely nothing, can separate you from God's love in Christ Jesus. Yes, God has an answer to the problem of suffering: His Son.

▼HINK ABOUT IT

Review the ways God works for good in suffering. Has God worked in your life in one of these ways? If so, how?

_____

_____

_____

_____

_____

---

[1]Kenneth Boa and Larry Moody, *I'm Glad You Asked* (Wheaton: Victor Books, 1982), 103-7.

[2]Mary Baker Eddy, *Science and Health with Key to the Scriptures* (Boston: Christian Science, 1903), 480.

[3]Boa and Moody, *I'm Glad You Asked*, 109.

[4]Norman L. Geisler, *The Roots of Evil* (Dallas: Probe Books, 1978), 26-28.

[5]Harold S. Kushner, *When Bad Things Happen to Good People* (New York: Schocken Books, 1981), 43.

[6]Ibid., 134.

[7]David B. Biebel, *If God Is So Good, Why Do I Hurt So Bad?* (Colorado Springs: NavPress, 1989), 19-20.

Reincarnation: The belief that every living thing does not die but changes forms, continuing to live in a new existence.

WHERE AM I GOING?

A final question must be considered: Where am I going? This question addresses life after death. As children we thought little about death or about life after death. It seemed distant and unreal. Then our naïveté was shattered by the death of a family member or a friend.

I will never forget the day my dad told me that my grandmother had died. I was returning from the store with my brother, riding double on his bike. I cried the rest of the way home, not understanding my own feelings. I remember visiting the funeral home and standing in line while people said that my grandmother looked good. I was confused because she didn't look good at all to me. She looked plastic. The animated smile that I had always seen on her face was missing. I didn't know what dead was supposed to look like, but I realized that this must be it.

"What will happen to Granny now?" I inquired. I was reassured that Granny was OK. She wasn't suffering anymore, I was told. Her body had worn out, and she had gone to be with Jesus. That explanation sufficed, and after a bout with grief, I accepted the reality of death, concluding that when you get old, you will die!

Just when I thought I had it all sorted out, the unexpected happened. A friend of mine ran into the street, was hit by a car, and died. Children aren't supposed to die! He wasn't old! Once again I was told that he was already in a better place; he was in heaven.

Through these circumstances I was introduced to the question, Where am I going? I did not know much about heaven and hell or about life after death, but I knew that heaven was the place I wanted to go. I knew that in heaven I could be with my grandmother and my buddy and that it was a wonderful place. Then I wanted to know how I could make sure that I would get to heaven after I died.

▼THINK ABOUT IT

When were you first confronted with the reality of death?

_____

_____

How were you affected?

_____

_____

Perhaps you are thinking that both my understanding and desire were childlike. You are right; they were. Yet for me—then and now—they answered the question, Where am I going? A recent *U.S. News and World Report* article indicates that I am not the only one who answers this question with reference to heaven and hell. According to this article, 78 percent of Americans believe in heaven, and 60 percent believe in hell. This contrasts with only 68 percent in 1965 who claimed to believe in heaven. Interestingly, only 4 percent think that they have an excellent or good chance of going to hell, while 78 percent think that they have an excellent or good chance of going to heaven.[1]

If our worldview is to be relevant, it must answer the question, Where am I going? It must also answer the corollary question, How do I get there? It is one thing to know where we want to go and quite another to know how to attain that goal. Nothing is more frustrating when driving than to know your destination but to be hopelessly lost, making no progress toward your ultimate goal. Thus, a worldview must offer meaningful answers to these two questions.

HOW DO THE WORLDVIEWS SEE OUR DESTINY?

Although most Americans would answer the question about our final destiny with a reference to heaven and hell, not all would. What are the other options? How do various worldviews deal with this critical issue?

Every worldview looks at history in a particular way. We can view history in only one of two ways. Either it is linear, with a beginning and an end, or it is cyclical, having neither a beginning nor an end. Carl F. H. Henry has written: "Our interim age is not open-ended; it carries an expiration date."[2] This has been and continues to be the predominant view of a majority of people in North America. Most of us believe that just as history had a beginning point, it also has an end. This is known as a linear view of history.

Yet the growing influence of Eastern thinking, with its roots in pantheism, particularly through the New Age movement, has challenged the linear view of history. Some would argue that history is cyclical, without beginning or end. Thus, while an individual might go through numerous stages of reincarnation, he will continue without end. With this in mind, let us look at different views of history to find their answers to the question, Where am I going?

Pantheism

How would a pantheist answer the question, Where am I going? He might respond that you do not need to worry about death because you will be reincarnated; you will have the opportunity to live many lifetimes. The word *reincarnate* means *to come again in the flesh*. Christians refer to the incarnation of Christ, which means that Christ came in human flesh. Pantheists believe that we will come back to life in different bodies even though our souls or spirits remain the same.

While this may sound foreign to some readers, reincarnation is growing in popularity, according to polls. Many well-known celebrities believe in reincarnation, perhaps the best known being Shirley MacLaine. In her book *Out on a Limb* she discusses her former incarnations, an understanding of which she gained through mediums. MacLaine has been joined by John Denver, Sylvester Stallone, and other Hollywood celebrities. Their high profile and access to the media have enabled them to teach reincarnation through television and movies. Reincarnation has been a theme in movies such as *Dead Again, Chances Are, The Reincarnation of Peter Proud,* and *The Reincarnate.*

How does reincarnation work? The human soul is believed to be immortal, surviving death as a mental entity. At death this soul enters a new embryo and brings with it all the karma of all its past lives. Karma is the law of cause and effect claiming that every decision an individual makes in the present is caused by all prior decisions and will thus affect every future decision. If a person's karma is evil, she will ultimately be reborn into a lower or less pleasant womb. Some believe that a person might come back even as an animal, a vegetable, or a mineral. If, however, one's karma is good, the individual enjoys the fruits of his good deeds, being born again into a new body appropriate to a new and higher realm of being.

The ultimate desire is to be freed from this cycle of reincarnation by becoming one with the divine Being. When this occurs, the soul loses all personal identity and becomes one with the One. This view depends on a belief in monism, that God is all and all is one. Thus, the human soul has always been one with God and must ultimately be reunited with the one divine Being.[3]

T HINK ABOUT IT

Define *reincarnation* in your own words.

_____

_____

Do you think reincarnation adequately answers the question,
Where am I going? Why or why not?

_____

_____

_____

Reincarnation fails to answer satisfactorily the question, Where am
I going? First, it simply delays the question for several lifetimes.
Second, what assurance do we have that anyone will ever live a
sufficient number of lifetimes to pay off the karmic debt of
previous failures? If we pay off some karmic debt yet incur new
karmic debt, what hope do we have that we will ever make it to
oneness with the One? Can we be assured that we will ever attain
to the infinite goodness of God? Finally, we must ask whether
impersonal absorption into the One (God) is a worthy goal and
satisfactory answer to the question, Where am I going?

Panentheism

Panentheism does not hold to a cyclical view of history but rather
claims that the universe itself is eternal. Because this worldview
tends to be more centered in the academic world, we have not
presented it in detail in this book. It views both God and the
universe as in process; both are evolving. Panentheists believe that
the universe (at least some universe) has always been and will
always be. The world is God's cosmic body, and the creatures of

the world are like cells in His body. Hence, the world and God are mutually dependent. The creatures of the universe contribute value to God. They enrich God and help Him fulfill what He lacks in perfection. Since God Himself is in process, it stands to reason that moral values themselves are not absolute but in flux. Persons have no personal immortality. Like all other creatures, they will die one day. Most panentheists believe that human destiny is to continue living in God's cosmic memory. If a person is good, he will have the satisfaction of knowing that God will remember him with fondness. Thus, although time goes on forever, individuals will die. A person's only hope is to live on in the memory of God, who is Himself incomplete.

This worldview has both an inadequate view of God and an unsatisfactory, impersonal answer to the question, Where am I going? I am going to die and cease to exist in a personal way. A person's memory will continue, but nothing else will. [4]

Atheism

The atheist believes that human beings are nothing more than matter. Because they have no immortal soul, when the body dies, the soul also dies. Some atheists speak of a collective immortality of the race or of the hope of an earthly paradise or utopia that will come through human effort. Of all the worldviews, atheism provides the most hopeless answers to the question about eternal destiny. Atheism can respond only that we are headed for death and dust.

Deism

The deist believes that history is linear and that the world did not exist until it was created by God. The universe now operates by natural laws that do not change and in which God does not intervene. The universe thus becomes the deist's Bible. Although God may be concerned about the affairs of human history, He does not involve Himself in them. Some deists argue that persons do not live after death; but others think that he survives death, although in an immaterial way. Martin Gardner, a 20th-century deist, believes in a personal afterlife in which one retains consciousness of identity and receives rewards and punishments for what is done on earth. He is not sure what this life will be like but is confident that the idea of eternal punishment should be rejected. Thus, he tends toward universalism. Although a deist holds a more hopeful view of life after death than adherents of the previous views, he has no sure answer. He rejects the special revelation from God by which we can know for sure what awaits us after death.

Theism

Three major world religions are often grouped in the broad category of theism: Judaism, Islam, and Christianity. All three share the conviction that after death the individual will live with God. Muslims believe that they will join Allah in heaven for an eternity of sensual pleasure and gratification. Some strains of Judaism believe that they will join the Messiah for a life in the hereafter. Other Jews believe that they will live on through their offspring, but they express little hope in life after death.

What is the viewpoint of Christianity, or biblical theism? Hebrews 9:27-28 gives a succinct answer to the question, Where am I going? "Just as man is destined to die once, and after that to face judgment, so Christ was sacrificed once to take away the sins of many people; and he will appear a second time, not to bear sin, but to bring salvation to those who are waiting for him." History is seen as linear, meaning that it has a clear and specific termination point that will be marked by Christ's return. All persons are destined to die and then to face judgment for their response to Christ.

THINK ABOUT IT
Label each tombstone with the name of the correct worldview.

That's all, folks!

1. _____

See you next time around!

2. _____

Who knows?

3. _____

Not here! Gone to be with God!

4. _____

Just a memory in the mind of God

5. _____

Answers: 1. atheism, 2. pantheism, 3. deism,
4. theism, 5. panentheism.

Through Christ, God has prepared a way for us to live forever. Let's take a closer look at the biblical view of where we are going after death.

The death of all humankind is ensured. Death entered human existence because of the human choice of sin (see Rom. 3:23).

All people will be resurrected from death. Resurrection is radically different from reincarnation. Reincarnation is the belief that after death the soul is reborn in another body. Resurrection is the teaching that after death the same physical body is made incorruptible. In 1 Corinthians 15 Paul discussed the resurrection of the body, noting that the glory of the resurrection body will far exceed that of the earthly body. Nevertheless, he made it abundantly clear that the perishable body that is sown is continuous with the imperishable one that is raised: "So will it be with the resurrection of the dead. The body that is sown is perishable, it is raised imperishable; it is sown in dishonor, it is raised in glory; it is sown in weakness, it is raised in power; it is sown a natural body, it is raised a spiritual body. If there is a natural body, there is also a spiritual body" (vv. 42-44).

While reincarnation is an intermediate step in a long process toward final absorption, resurrection, as taught in the Bible, is the perfect and final state for humankind.

Judgment and eternity await all people. Revelation 20 speaks of two resurrections, one to life and another to judgment:

> I saw thrones on which were seated those who had
> been given authority to judge. And I saw the souls
> of those who had been beheaded because of their
> testimony for Jesus and because of the word of
> God. They had not worshiped the beast or his
> image and had not received his mark on their
> foreheads or their hands. They came to life and
> reigned with Christ a thousand years. (The rest of

the dead did not come to life until the thousand
years were ended.) This is the first resurrection.
Blessed and holy are those who have part in the
first resurrection. The second death has no power
over them, but they will be priests of God and of
Christ and will reign with him for a thousand years
(vv. 4-6).

The first resurrection involves only those over whom the second
death has no power. These will be resurrected to spend eternity
reigning with Him. The second resurrection occurs later, as verses
11-15 make clear:

> Then I saw a great white throne and him who was
> seated on it. Earth and sky fled from his presence,
> and there was no place for them. And I saw the
> dead, great and small, standing before the throne,
> and books were opened. Another book was
> opened, which is the book of life. The dead were
> judged according to what they had done as
> recorded in the books. The sea gave up the dead
> that were in it, and death and Hades gave up the
> dead that were in them, and each person was
> judged according to what he had done. Then death
> and Hades were thrown into the lake of fire. The
> lake of fire is the second death. If anyone's name
> was not found written in the book of life, he was
> thrown into the lake of fire.

This judgment will be based on deeds; thus, it is entirely just. The
dilemma is that no one will be found righteous according to his
deeds. The whole of Scripture points to the dilemma of judgment
based on deeds. For example, in Romans 3 Paul clearly painted the

picture of the human dilemma when he declared that both Jews and Greeks were under sin. To prove his point, he quoted from the Old Testament: " 'There is no one righteous, not even one; there is no one who understands, no one who seeks God. All have turned away, they have together become worthless; there is no one who does good, not even one' " (vv. 10-12).

Since the human predicament could not be answered by human accomplishments, God provided a way for persons to be forgiven of their sin and to stand before Him in judgment: " 'God so loved the world, that he gave his one and only Son, that whoever believes in him shall not perish but have eternal life. . . . Whoever believes in him is not condemned, but whoever does not believe stands condemned already because he has not believed in the name of God's one and only Son' " (John 3:16-18). God did not ignore our sin; He paid the penalty for our sin. Jesus, who lived without sin, bore the penalty of our sin, dying in our place. Since He was sinless, He did not need to die to pay for His own sin. His death was a voluntary sacrifice to pay the penalty for our sin (see John 10:17-18).

▼THINK ABOUT IT

How would you respond if a friend asked you what it means to say that Christ died for our sin?

_____

_____

_____

_____

_____

_____

When you realize that Christ died for your sin, how do you feel?

_____

_____

_____

God's demand for justice was satisfied by Jesus' sacrificial death in our place. Therefore, we are saved by God's unmerited grace. When we stand before God, we need grace, not justice. Grace is received in a personal relationship with Christ, who Himself paid the penalty for our sin. Revelation 20:15 accurately declares, "If anyone's name was not found written in the book of life, he was thrown into the lake of fire." This means that no one whose name is not written in the book of life will escape the second death. No one will be saved by works. Only those who have received the forgiveness of sin through Christ's grace will have their names inscribed in the book of life.

All people will be resurrected in immortal bodies. The only question is whether they will be resurrected to spend eternity with God, enjoying His fellowship forever, or separated from Him forever in the lake of fire. A person's answer to, Where am I going? depends on his own free choice to receive God's free gift of heaven. God does not send anyone to hell, but He gives each person the result of his choice.

If you choose Christ, here is what is in store for you after death: "Praise be to the God and Father of our Lord Jesus Christ! In his great mercy he has given us new birth into a living hope through the resurrection of Jesus Christ from the dead, and into an inheritance that can never perish, spoil or fade—kept in heaven for you, who through faith are shielded by God's power until the coming of the salvation that is ready to be revealed in the last time" (1 Pet. 1:3-5).

▼**THINK ABOUT IT**

Answer the following questions.

1. Do you often think about what actually happens to a person at death? Yes ____ No ____

2. Have you ever personally witnessed a person's death? Yes ____ No ____ If so, describe your feelings about that experience.

_____

_____

_____

_____

3. Do you believe that a heaven exists? Yes ____ No ____ Uncertain ____

4. Do you believe that a hell exists?
Yes ____ No ____ Uncertain ____

5. Do you know where you are going after this life?
Yes ____ No ____ Uncertain ____

HOW DO I GET THERE?

At the beginning of this chapter we suggested that any worldview must adequately answer the question, How do I get to my ultimate destination? When we examine all worldviews, we ultimately discover only two options: works and grace.

An atheist, of course, doesn't attempt to answer this question because he is all dressed up with nowhere to go. All other worldviews attempt to answer this question with good works. A pantheist or a New Age adherent may embellish their answers with words like *enlightenment.* But ultimately, reincarnation is an effort to repay karmic debt, which is attempted through good works.

A Jew believes that he will reach heaven by living a moral life and by obeying God's law. A Muslim attempts to earn salvation by believing in the five doctrines of Islam and by performing the duties of the Five Pillars of Faith. Although various worldviews may state it differently, the answer to how one gets there is always the same—good works. But none of these views can ensure salvation because it is impossible to know for certain that one has accumulated a sufficient number of good works to atone for sins. These major religious groups, along with such Eastern religions as Hinduism and Buddhism, all seek to answer the question, How do I get there? with some form of human effort.[5]

Only the Christian worldview insists that our salvation rests solely in God's provision and grace. Persons enter heaven based on whether they have chosen to accept Christ's payment on the cross for their sin. Human achievement plays no part in our entrance into heaven. It is important to understand this distinctive. Many persons who consider themselves Christians often answer the question, How do I get there? with a works answer. Phrases like "I'm a good person," "I believe in God," and "I belong to a Christian church" testify to the large number of confessed Christians who plan to get into heaven based on their works.

THINK ABOUT IT

What word best describes the methods all religions except Christianity use to seek eternal life?

What word describes the way a Christian receives eternal life?

To make sure this issue is clear in your mind, let's look at a simple answer to the question, How do I get there?

> As for you, you were dead in your transgressions and sins, in which you used to live when you followed the ways of this world and of the ruler of the kingdom of the air, the spirit who is now at work in those who are disobedient. All of us also lived among them at one time, gratifying the cravings of our sinful nature and following its desires and thoughts. Like the rest, we were by nature objects of wrath. But because of his great love for us, God, who is rich in mercy, made us alive with Christ even when we were dead in transgressions—it is by grace you have been saved. And God raised us up with Christ and seated us with him in the heavenly realms in Christ Jesus, in order that in the coming ages he might show the incomparable riches of his grace, expressed in his kindness to us in Christ Jesus. For it is by grace you have been saved, through faith—and this not from yourselves, it is the gift of God—not by works, so that no one can boast. For we are God's workmanship, created in Christ Jesus to do good works, which God prepared in advance for us to do (Eph. 2:1-10).

Paul began with a statement of the human dilemma: "You were dead in your transgressions and sins" (v. 1). Humans were created as living beings in God's image so that they might have relationships with God and with other persons. But all persons, like Adam, choose sin. The result of that sin is alienation from holy God. This separation or alienation from God is often called death in the New Testament. Because of their sin, persons are spiritually dead.

As a result of our sins, Paul called us disobedient (see v. 2), driven by the desires of our flesh and mind (see v. 3). Without God a person lives a human-centered life, ruled by desires and passions. As a result, without divine intervention we all would be children of wrath, and our eternal destiny would be separation from God.

This result is not God's design or desire. Note how Paul stated it: "Because of his great love for us, God, who is rich in mercy, made us alive with Christ even when we were dead in transgressions—it is by grace you have been saved" (vv. 4-5). God's desire is to seat us with Him in the heavenly places in Christ Jesus and to show us "the incomparable riches of his grace, expressed in his kindness to us in Christ Jesus" (v. 7).

How can all this happen if we are separated from God because of our sins? Paul explained, "It is by grace you have been saved, through faith—and this not from yourselves, it is the gift of God—not by works, so that no one can boast" (vv. 8-9). We receive God's free gift of eternal life when we acknowledge our need, turn from our own way, and receive the free gift of grace by inviting Christ to be our Savior.

The result of this wonderful decision will be not only eternal life in heaven but also empowered living in the present. Notice verse 10 of this same passage: "We are God's workmanship, created in Christ Jesus to do good works, which God prepared in advance for us to do." When we receive the free gift of eternal life, we are not only assured of heaven for eternity but also enabled to live in a meaningful way.

The following chart illustrates the two basic worldview options, works and grace.

WORKS OR GRACE?

Works	Grace
• Human initiative	• God's initiative
• Sinful humans reaching up to God	• Holy God reaching down to sinful humans
• Never quite sure	• Confident in Jesus' sacrifice
• Outward devotion	• Inward change
• No relationship with God	• Intimate relationship with God
• Being good	• Being in Christ
• Worry	• Great confidence
• Continual attempts to pay off debt of sin	• Debt paid in full by Jesus Christ
• Most world religions	• Christianity alone
• Laws to follow	• Person (Jesus) to follow
• Hope centered in human goodness	• Hope centered in God's goodness
• Frustrated, guilty	• Peace, forgiveness
• Penitence	• Atonement
• Legalism	• Mercy

THINK ABOUT IT

In your opinion, why do people trust works for their salvation?

_____

_____

_____

IS THE CHRISTIAN WORLDVIEW NARROW?

Christians are often asked this question. In chapter 1 we noted that by definition only one worldview can be correct. If one worldview answers all of life's questions with unity and integrity, then it alone must be correct. We have evaluated various worldviews in our attempt to answer life's most pressing problems. Only the Christian worldview provided consistent answers to all of the problems.

Any worldview is of necessity narrow. Any worldview or religious system claims to be the right way to live, thus creating exclusivity for itself. Atheists claim to be right in asserting that God does not exist, and they have little tolerance for those who differ from that view. Jews, Buddhists, and Muslims all believe that they have found the only true way to God. On the surface, some worldviews appear to allow for different ways, but on closer examination they all demand exclusivity. When children of Muslims or Hindus want to become Christians, the exclusivity of these systems quickly becomes apparent.

The various worldviews offer radically different and often contradictory answers to questions about our origin, purpose, and destiny. Too much is at stake to give up and argue that all of the views are right or wrong. Just because three of four answers to a math problem may be wrong does not mean that we should throw out the fourth answer.

Truth is exclusive by definition. We do not think it narrow-minded to say that 2 plus 2 always equals 4 and not 3.5 or 4.2. When I fly on an airplane, I am not disconcerted that the navigator or pilot takes a narrow approach to the navigational setting for my flight. The runway is my destination, and I know that we will not arrive safely if the plane is off course by even a single degree.

THINK ABOUT IT
Complete this sentence: By definition truth is _____.

The claims of the Christian worldview are narrow. We know this from Christ's claims about Himself. Read these verses from John's Gospel and note the exclusivity of Christ's claim.

> "Whoever believes in him is not condemned, but whoever does not believe stands condemned already because he has not believed in the name of God's one and only Son" (John 3:18).

> "I told you that you would die in your sins; if you do not believe that I am the one I claim to be, you will indeed die in your sins" (John 8:24).

> Jesus answered, "I am the way and the truth and the life. No one comes to the Father except through me" (John 14:6).

> Jesus answered: "Don't you know me, Philip, even after I have been among you such a long time? Anyone who has seen me has seen the Father. How can you say, 'Show us the Father'?" (John 14:9).

Jesus often used the title I AM to refer to Himself. This title was the name by which God revealed Himself to Moses in Exodus 3:14. Thus, Jesus was claiming that He was God. For example, He referred to His eternal existence in John 8:58 by stating: " 'I tell you the truth, . . . before Abraham was born, I am!' " His hearers understood the significance of this claim, as verse 59 makes clear: "At this, they picked up stones to stone him, but Jesus hid himself, slipping away from the temple grounds." They wanted to stone

Him for blasphemy.

In a similar I AM saying in John 8:24 Jesus claimed to come from heaven and to be able to forgive sins: " 'I told you that you would die in your sins; if you do not believe that I am the one I claim to be, you will indeed die in your sins.' "

The early church continued this insistence that Christ is the exclusive way to God. Acts 4 recounts the arrest of Peter and John for teaching the people about the resurrection from the dead available only in Jesus (see v. 2). In his defense Peter reiterated that he had done his mighty deeds by the power of Jesus Christ the Nazarene, whom they had crucified and whom God had raised from the dead. Then he declared in verse 12: " 'Salvation is found in no one else, for there is no other name under heaven given to men by which we must be saved.' "

John began his Gospel by referring to Christ's preexistence and then declared, "To all who received him, to those who believed in his name, he gave the right to become children of God—children born not of natural descent, nor of human decision or a husband's will, but born of God" (1:12-13).

▼THINK ABOUT IT

Have you ever been criticized for being narrow-minded as a Christian? Yes ____   No ____

If so, how did you feel?

_____

_____

_____

_____

_____

Now that you have read the previous section, list responses you would make to such an accusation.

_____

_____

_____

_____

_____

Throughout our study we have noticed the failings of the alternative worldviews to answer some of the critical questions of life. Now we must ask whether the Christian worldview passes the five tests of sufficiency, unity, consistency, integrity, and practical relevance.

CHRISTIANITY PASSES THE TESTS

☑ The Christian worldview passes the test of sufficiency because it provides sufficient and valid answers to all of life's critical questions.

☑ The Christian worldview passes the test of unity because it demands that we integrate all of our thinking about life with the teachings of the revealed Word of God.

☑ The Christian worldview passes the test of consistency, as we have seen throughout this book.

☑ The Christian worldview passes the test of integrity because it does not require the believer to ignore known facts, nor does it require us to invent facts.

☑ The Christian worldview is relevant because it deals with the issues of everyday living.

▼**T**HINK ABOUT IT

Reread each test statement. If you are ready to affirm that
Christianity passes the test, write your initials beside it in this list.

____ Sufficiency
____ Unity
____ Consistency
____ Integrity
____ Practical relevance

If you have never received Christ as your personal Savior, you
can do so right now. Simply acknowledge your sinfulness and your
inability to rid yourself of it. Receive Christ as the payment for
your sin by inviting Him to come into your life and to forgive
your sin. Commit your whole being to follow Him as a learner.
Follow through on this commitment by identifying with His body,
which is the local church. Make public your commitment to
Christ in a Bible-teaching fellowship of believers.

If you know Christ, you must dedicate yourself to His service.
Make sure that all of your thoughts, decisions, and actions are
consistent with the teachings of God's Word and with the Holy
Spirit's leadership in your life. Live your life in a way that testifies
to your distinctive Christian worldview, recognizing that your
purpose is to bring glory to God through all eternity. Introduce
others to Christ so that they too may spend eternity with the
Father.

▼**T**HINK ABOUT IT

List steps you will take to identify with Christ, to grow in Him,
and to serve Him.

_____

_____

_____

Now that you have completed this study, write your own worldview.

MY WORLDVIEW

Now compare your statements with the worldview you wrote in chapter 1. How has this study changed your view of life?

_____

_____

_____

_____

_____

_____

_____

_____

_____

_____

_____

[1]"Hell's Sober Comeback," *U.S. News and World Report*, 25 March 1991, 57.

[2]Carl F. H. Henry, *The Christian Mindset in a Secular Society* (Multnomah: Oregon, 1984), 44.

[3]For a more complete discussion of reincarnation and resurrection, read Norman L. Geisler and Ronald M. Brooks, *When Skeptics Ask* (Wheaton: Victor Books, 1990), 233-54, or Norman L. Geisler and William D. Watkins, *Worlds Apart* (Grand Rapids: Baker Book House, 1989), 83-84.

[4]For more information on panentheism, see Norman L. Geisler and William D. Watkins, *Worlds Apart* (Grand Rapids: Baker Book House, 1989), 107-46.

[5]Kenneth Boa and Larry Moody, *I'm Glad You Asked* (Wheaton: Victor Books, 1982), 133-34.

150

Boa, Kenneth, and Larry Moody. *I'm Glad You Asked.* Wheaton: Victor Books, 1982.

Bush, L. Russ. *A Handbook for Christian Philosophy.* Grand Rapids: Zondervan, 1991.

Geisler, Norman L., and Ronald M. Brooks. *When Skeptics Ask.* Wheaton: Victor Books, 1990.

Gill, Jerry H. *On Knowing God: Directions for the Future of Theology.* Philadelphia: Westminster, 1981.

Henry, Carl F. H. *The Christian Mindset in a Secular Society.* Portland: Multnomah, 1984.

_____. *Toward a Recovery of Christian Belief.* Wheaton: Crossway Books, 1990.

Holmes, Arthur F. *Contours of a World View.* Grand Rapids: Eerdmans, 1983.

Kennedy, D. James. *Why I Believe.* Dallas: Word, 1980.

Little, Paul. *Know Why You Believe.* Downers Grove: InterVarsity, 1968.

CHRISTIAN GROWTH STUDY PLAN

Preparing Christians to Serve

In the **Christian Growth Study Plan (formerly Church Study Course),** this book
is a resource for course credit in the subject area
of the Christian Growth category of diploma plans. To receive credit, read the book, complete the learning activities, show your work to your pastor, a staff member or church leader, then complete the information on the next page. The form may be duplicated. Send the completed page to:

Christian Growth Study Plan
127 Ninth Avenue, North, MSN 117
Nashville, TN 37234-0117
FAX: (615)251-5067

For information about the Christian Growth Study Plan, refer to the current Christian Growth Study Plan Catalog. Your church office may have a copy. If not, request a free copy from the Christian Growth Study Plan office (615/251-2525).

LifeAnswers: Making Sense of Your World
CG-0151

PARTICIPANT INFORMATION

Social Security Number (USA ONLY)

Personal CGSP Number*

Date of Birth (MONTH, DAY, YEAR)

Name (First, Middle, Last)
☐ Mr. ☐ Miss
☐ Mrs.

Home Phone

Address (Street, Route, or P.O. Box)

City, State, or Province

Zip/Postal Code

CHURCH INFORMATION

Church Name

Address (Street, Route, or P.O. Box)

City, State, or Province

Zip/Postal Code

CHANGE REQUEST ONLY

☐ Former Name

☐ Former Address

City, State, or Province

Zip/Postal Code

☐ Former Church

City, State, or Province

Zip/Postal Code

Signature of Pastor, Conference Leader, or Other Church Leader

Date

*New participants are requested but not required to give SS# and date of birth. Existing participants, please give CGSP# when using SS# for the first time. Thereafter, only one ID# is required. **Mail to:** Christian Growth Study Plan, 127 Ninth Ave., North, Nashville, TN 37234-0117. Fax: (615)251-5067

Generation X'ers — Making Life's Journey Count

Generation X. Who are they? What makes them tick? This generation, though in conflict with itself and others, is filled with great potential. An individualistic, in-your-face group, X'ers want their leaders to be authentic, credible, willing to share their own struggles and feelings, contemporary and humorous in their approach, concise with biblical texts, and ready to provide concrete examples for living the Christian life.

David Edwards, a gifted communicator, provides all of these in *Destination: Principles for Making Life's Journey Count*, a video-based study for young adults. Resources include the following:

- 4, 45-minute VHS videos - available separately for $19.95 each
  The Road Ahead (Item #0-7673-2663-6)
  Signs That You Don't Get It (Item #0-7673-2664-4)
  Enjoy the Ride (Item #0-7673-2665-2)
  Getting to Your Destination (Item #0-7673-2666-0)
- *Destination: Principles for Making Life's Journey Count Member Workbook* - $5.95
- *Destination: Principles for Making Life's Journey Count* Leader Kit (includes all four videos, the member workbook, and a leader guide) - $79.95

Destination can be used in a variety of settings such as a weekend retreat, a 4-week study, or an 8-week study. Destination is high-energy and contemporary—guaranteed to appeal to Generation X'ers!

Destination: Principles for Making Life's Journey Count resources can be ordered in any of the following ways: PHONE 1-800-458-2772; FAX (615) 251-5933; EMAIL customerservice@bssb.com; WRITE Customer Service Center, 127 Ninth Avenue North, Nashville, TN 37234-0113; or VISIT the nearest Baptist Book Store or Lifeway Christian Store serving you.